Dedication

This book is dedicated to our son Scott.

Scott used to spend a lot of time in the garage fiddling around with his old Suburu station wagon. Learning how to upgrade an old computer is my way of spending time in the garage.

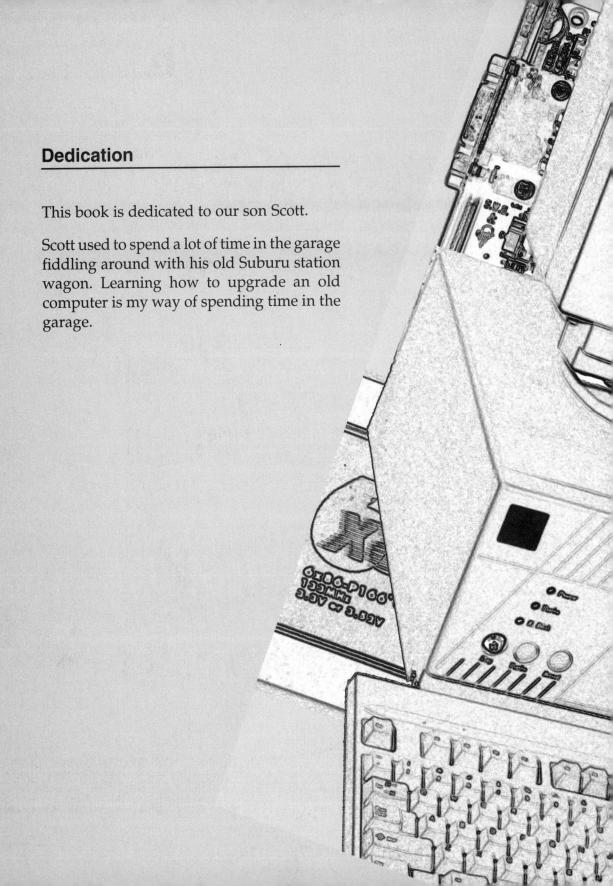

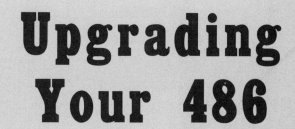

Upgrading
Your 486

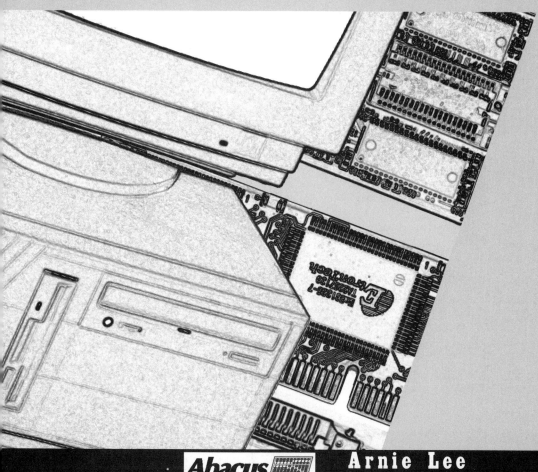

Abacus Arnie Lee
www.abacuspub.com

Copyright © 1997   **Abacus**
5370 52nd Street SE
Grand Rapids, MI 49512

www.abacuspub.com

Printed in the U.S.A.

ISBN 1-55755-323-8

10 9 8 7 6 5 4 3 2 1

Table Of Contents

Table Of Contents

Table Of Contents

Introduction

Introduction

Here's a common scenario for many computer users in recent times:

"You've been waiting for just the right time to buy your dream PC. You've studied the specs and have carefully shopped around to make sure you're getting the best system for your hard earned money. Finally, you take the big plunge. You plop your plastic money onto the computer dealer's checkout counter and carry home a new Intel 486 speedster. It has a great big hard drive, a super fast modem and more memory than you've ever had before.

"So there you are, enjoying your new PC. You're treating it like man's best friend. But in just a few short months, you see the announcement that makes your heart sink. The brand new Pentium CPU threatens to make your expensive 486 system obsolete."

Yes, this is a very common scene. The pace at which computer technology is changing is so rapid, that it's hard to know what is the best system to buy at any given moment. Technology is a two-edged sword. As it delivers great products, it obsoletes others.

One great thing about our economy is that competition helps to push through advances in technology. This is one of the reasons why Pentium-class CPUs have taken over the desktop marketplace in such a short period of time. They're fast, reliable and pervasive. In fact, very few computer manufacturers make those "ancient" 486's. They've all switched to making Pentium computers.

So what do you do with your 486 that was last year's state of the art system? You've invested thousands of dollars into this computer and have probably filled it to the brim with peripherals, add-ons, software and love and care.

Chances are that you can retain a significant amount of your original investment if you care to roll up your sleeves and upgrade your 486.

Why upgrade?

Do any of these descriptions apply to you?

❖ You feel inadequate because your next door neighbor or fellow worker has a Pentium screamer.

❖ You are tired of drinking coffee while waiting for your graphics to redraw on the screen.

❖ You feel that Windows 95 was named for the number of seconds that you have to wait until a new window opens.

❖ You bought the winning lotto ticket last week, but misplaced it on the way to collect the winnings.

❖ You have a real guilty feeling about environmental waste issues and feel that it would be politically incorrect to toss it out.

❖ You'd like to add a new peripheral, but aren't sure if it will be compatible with your next generation computer.

Yes, there are many reasons why you might want to upgrade that 486 of yours rather than buying a new one. But the reason most often stated is to save money. Even lotto winners know that they can use the savings from upgrading a 486 to buy more tickets for the next drawing.

Since you're reading this book, we assume that you're truly interested saving a wad by upgrading your 486. In the next few chapters, we'll show you how.

However, before doing so, we'd like to set a few ground rules. Here's what we mean by upgrading your 486:

❖ Install a new motherboard and Pentium-class CPU

❖ Install a new video card

❖ Install new memory (if 72-pin SIMMS aren't already installed)

❖ Retain your original hard drive

❖ Retain your original CD-ROM drive

❖ Retain your original floppy drive

❖ Retain your original modem

❖ Retain your original network interface card

❖ Retain your original sound card

❖ Retain your original case

❖ Retain your original keyboard

❖ Retain your original mouse

❖ Retain your original monitor

❖ Retain your original operating system

If you look at the list above, you'll notice that we have added only a few new components. All of the other components are from your original system. This is one of the reasons that you'll save money by upgrading.

How much can you save?

This is a difficult question to answer. You can look through the newspapers and computer magazines to determine how much a comparable new system costs. Perhaps a better way to express this is "how much will this upgrade cost?" By answering this question, you can determine if you would rather spend this amount to upgrade your 486 or spend a larger amount to purchase a comparable brand new system.

We bought the following components to upgrade several 486 computers:

❖ P54C motherboard with Triton chipset ($160)

❖ Intel P-133 CPU with fan   *or*

  Cyrix P-150+ CPU with fan ($225)

❖ PCI-bus VGA card ($ 75)

Notice that we didn't have to buy additional RAM because our 486 already had 16MB of 72-pin SIMMs. We'll be able to upgrade this 486 system for a very reasonable cost.

The prices here are "street prices" for components that you can buy from a computer dealer, superstore or trade show.

Can my 486 system be upgraded?

For most of you, the answer is yes. Most 486 computers can be easily upgraded to a Pentium.

There are exceptions of course. Some computer manufacturers have designed their systems to save space. These compact units have specially designed motherboards that cannot easily be replaced. Why not? Because the original motherboard is nonstandard, so a replacement motherboard may not fit in the allotted space in the computer system's case. To upgrade these systems, you may have to replace the case which in turn increases the cost of upgrading slightly. However, you can replace the case and still use many of the other components from your 486 and still save money.

In a short while, we'll show you how to determine if you can use your existing case or will have to buy a new one.

Am I capable of upgrading my 486 system?

We have demonstrated to many different users how they can upgrade their 486es. These users have ranged from a 10-year old girl to experienced electronic technicians. In each case, they have successfully completed the task.

If we could show you in person how to upgrade your 486, then the answer is definitely yes. However in this book, we have to rely on our ability to explain the upgrade process in words, photos and illustrations. If we aren't skillful enough in our explanations, then it's possible that you could run into trouble. But we don't intend to let you down.

We assume that your 486 system has these minimum characteristics:

- ❖ IDE hard drive
- ❖ Floppy drive
- ❖ VGA monitor
- ❖ Serial or PS/2 style mouse

Why is it so easy to upgrade?

The answer is — *standardization*. Let's explain this a little further.

As you know, the Pentium CPU is made by Intel Corporation. Early in the life cycle of the Pentium, Intel urged all of the manufacturers of PC components to standardize their products. By standardizing, these components would function more or less interchangeably.

Furthermore, standardization would lead to lower prices since smaller component makers would be assured that their designs were compatible with those from larger manufacturers. Intel made sure that other manufacturers got the message about standardization by itself becoming a manufacturer of some of these components. This led other component manufacturers to follow Intel's lead.

Thanks to standardization, it's not surprising that large number of components can now be used as building blocks for Pentium computers. This in turn makes is quite easy to upgrade a 486 to a Pentium.

What is the goal of this book?

We'd like to show the average consumer, who may not be an electronics whiz, how to turn a 486 computer into a state-of-the-art Pentium. Along the way you'll retain a considerable amount of your initial investment in your original 486 system and learn a lot more about how it functions.

This book is a practical, hand-on guide to upgrading. You can't upgrade a computer without getting your hands dirty — or at least a little soiled.

We'll try to go easy on the theory and go heavy on the "how-to."

We aren't going to do a complete makeover of your 486 computer system. Rather we're going to show you how to replace the "engine" of your computer. To put it in other words, if we were cardiac specialists, we'd be performing a heart transplant. These doctors don't usually perform joint replacements and neither will we show you how to change your CD-ROM or hard drive. If you need to upgrade these components, you may want to read one of the books listed in Chapter 6.

Anyway, let's get on with the new "engine."

The Components
Of A Computer

Chapter 1

Chapter 1

The Components Of A Computer

In some ways, the personal computer is similar to the automobile. There are many different makes and models of automobiles. Some autos have small, economy engines and others have large and very powerful engines; some have AM/FM radios, others tape cassette decks and still others CD players; some have standard suspensions and others have heavy duty towing packages. But regardless of the options which you buy, automobiles are basically used for transportation.

(Figure 1.1) Some autos are built for speed ...and so are some computers

Similarly, there are many makes and models of personal computers. Some have economy priced CPUs and others have faster, more expensive CPUs; some have a minimal 4MB of memory and others are loaded with a generous 32MB; some have low-cost 2X CD-ROM drives and others speedy 10X drives; some have 14.4KBPS modems and others the latest 33.6KBPS voice-response modems. But regardless of the features, PCs are basically used to run applications.

The components which you choose to put into your PC are similar to the options which you choose for your automobile. Choosing different components determines how your PC performs just as choosing various options determines how your automobile performs.

Selecting the right components is important for two reasons:

1. Choosing components ultimately determines how your PC performs.

2. Choosing components also determines how much your PC costs.

One of our objectives it to help you to save money. But it isn't wise to save money only to get inferior quality. We're planning to show you how to build a quality computer system.

Examine your budget, use a prepared shopping list and accept only straight answers to the questions that you ask your sales person. Buy what you need, not what the store or vendor has to sell. If you follow these guidelines, you'll save money and build the PC that meets your needs.

A BARE BONES COMPUTER

It's not our intention to bore you with "old" information, but it may be helpful to look at the makeup of a computer system. Let's look at the components in a "stripped down" computer—the minimum components that all personal computers are made from:

Case

This is the box or shell in which all of the other components are assembled. The case is typically made of metal, plastic or a combination of the two. We'll be reusing the case from your 486.

Power supply

An enclosed metallic box which regulates the electrical power for the other components. Usually the power supply is pre-installed in the case. We assume that your case has the power supply built-in.

CPU

This is an acronym for "Central Processing Unit" which is the brain of your PC. Choosing a CPU is the single most important factor in how powerful your upgraded PC will be. We'll be replacing your 486 CPU with a Pentium-class processor.

CPU cooling fan

This is a small assembly with a fan that sits on top of the CPU to remove the heat generated by the processor.

Motherboard

The motherboard is a large circuit board which "accepts" most of the other components. The CPU, memory, video cards, hard, floppy and CD-ROM drives and other input/output cards plug into the motherboard.

Memory

Memory is used as working storage for all programs. The memory is contained on small plug-in cards often called as SIMMs. This stands for Single Inline Memory Module, which is a fancy name for the way in which the memory is packaged on small circuit boards. A new style of module is the DIMM, for Dual Inline Memory Module, which is not yet commonly used and is significantly more expensive than a SIMM.

Video display card

This is a small plug-in card containing specialized chips which generate the signals for displaying text and graphics on the video monitor.

Monitor

This is a video display device (looking like a television) on which the text and graphics appear.

I/O board

An I/O board is another small plug-in card. This one contains the electronics which control the hard drives, floppy drives, communication ports, printer port and game port. There are two major types of I/O boards, IDE and SCSI. In this book we'll refer only to IDE controllers and not the more expensive SCSI controllers.

Floppy drive

This is a small storage device that reads and writes from/to floppy disks.

Hard drive

This is a storage device for holding megabytes (millions of bytes) or gigabytes (billions of bytes) of information. A hard drive not only has more capacity than a floppy drive, but reads and writes the data dozens of times faster.

Keyboard

The device that lets you to type information into the computer.

Many readers are under the impression that a computer is a complex piece of equipment. In fact, it's not at all complex. To show you that it's actually quite simple, the computer system in Figure 1.2 is put together on the top of a table so you can see that there are very few connections involved. We used all of the components listed above (except for the case) to make this "bare bones" computer system. You can connect the components together like this in a few minutes.

(Figure 1.2) This computer was assembled on the top of a table to show you that there aren't very many connections.

Our tabletop computer is a real working computer system. It runs just like one enclosed in a case. However, we don't recommend that you upgrade your 486 computer on the top of a table. One of the hazards of doing this is that it's easy to short circuit the motherboard or one of the add-on cards when you don't have a case to protect the components. Short circuiting a delicate component will probably ruin it.

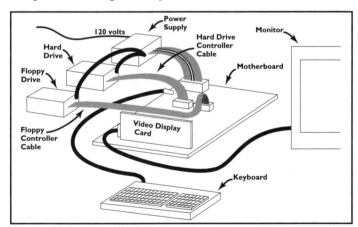

(Figure 1.3) This diagram shows how the components in Figure 1.2 are connected.

A STATE OF THE ART "SCREAMER"

The tabletop computer will not satisfy any of you since it is really a bare bones PC. But it's quite easy to turn this basic machine into a state-of-the-art computer by adding a few features, such as the ones we've listed below. These components will turn a basic PC system into a real Pentium screamer:

CD-ROM drive

This is a storage device which reads CD-ROMs, circular plastic discs, that are used to hold programs and information. Able to hold up to 650MB of information, CD-ROMs provide an economical and convenient way to distribute large programs and huge amounts of data.

Sound card

This is a plug-in card which can capture, digitize and playback sound. The sound may be music, voices or effects in either monaural or stereo.

Speakers

These are similar or identical to audio stereo speakers for amplifying and/or playing the digitized sound generated by a sound card.

Modem

This is a plug-in card (or in the case of an external modem, a small box) which converts digital information into a form that can be sent back and forth over ordinary telephone lines. A modem is used to connect one computer to another computer in a different location.

Tape backup

This is a storage device that uses small plastic tape cartridges. The cartridges are used to store data that is originally written to the hard drive. By copying or backing up the data from the hard drive to the tape cartridge, the data is preserved in case the original data on the hard drive is destroyed.

Mouse

This is a small hand device used to interact with the graphical user interfaces such as Windows 3.x and Windows 95.

Other peripherals

There are many other peripherals or devices that you can attach to your PC. These includes printers, scanners, zip drives, bar code readers and the list goes on. Since installing most of these other peripherals is straightforward and has little to do with building your PC, we'll leave it to others to explain.

YOUR LEGACY 486 COMPUTER SYSTEM

We've seen that all computers are made from only a few basic components.

Your computer system has a CPU designated by the name "486." This is a generic name for a chip that was probably manufactured by Intel or one of the clone manufacturers, AMD or Cyrix.

The name 486 covers a wide range of CPUs. Among them are the 486SX, 486 SX2, 486DX, 486DX2, 486DX4 and 486SL. They differ in CPU speed, bus speed, bus width, power consumption and other factors.

Luckily, these differences aren't relevant to what we're going to do. We're going to totally disregard the type of CPU that's in your current system. We're going to replace it with a Pentium-class CPU.

We'll be replacing the following components from the "Bare Bones" section of the chapter:

❖ Motherboard

❖ CPU

❖ CPU Cooling Fan

❖ Video Display Card

❖ Memory

Before we upgrade our 486, we'll first have to purchase these components. Chapter 2 is devoted to just this topic. There we describe in detail what factors you'll want to consider in selecting the above components.

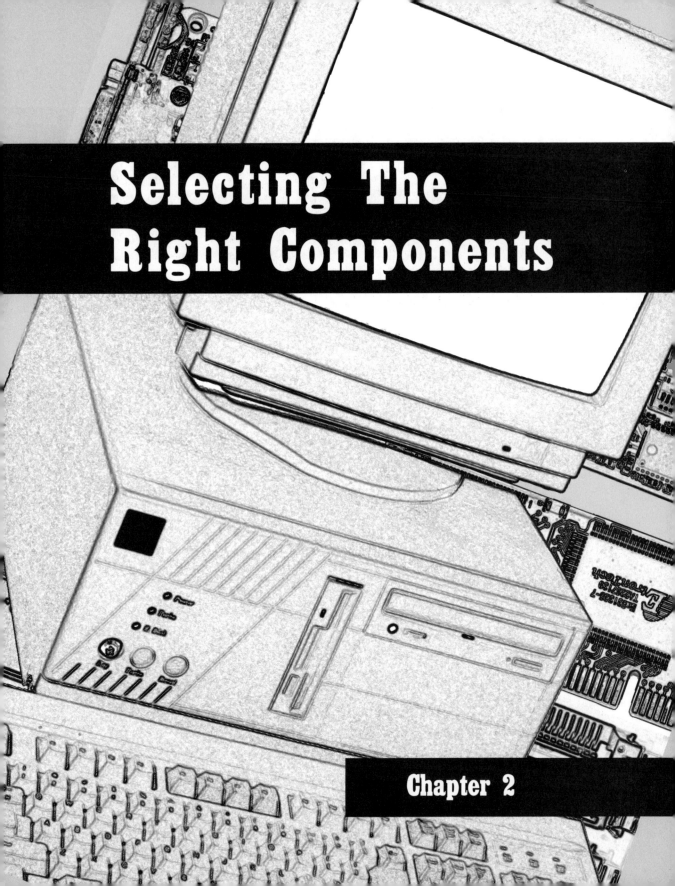

Selecting The Right Components

Chapter 2

Chapter 2

Selecting The Right Components

For many users, the most confusing and time-consuming part of upgrading their computer system is selecting the components. There are many factors to consider when buying components and when you start shopping for them, you may be bewildered by the myriad of choices available in every component category. Don't worry. We're going to get you started in the right direction.

Here are some of the factors that you'll want to consider when shopping for the components to build your computer:

THE CPU

To repeat what we said earlier, the single most important factor in the performance of your upgraded computer system is which CPU you choose. For Pentium-class performance, there are really only two manufacturers that you can turn to: Intel and Cyrix.

The Pentium line of CPUs is available only from Intel Corporation. The Cyrix Corporation makes the C6x86 line of CPUs which are functionally equivalent to Intel's Pentiums. Independent testing organizations have verified that for general applications, the 686 line offers better performance than the Intel CPUs at a comparable price. We won't argue the merits of

23

choosing an Intel Pentium over a Cyrix C6x86 processor. Let's just say that we have upgraded many computers with Intel Pentiums and with Cyrix C6x86es and have experienced great performance improvements with chips from either manufacturer.

Selecting the "right" CPU is a tradeoff between price and performance. Let's talk about performance.

The power rating of a CPU is based on its *clock speed*. Here's why: the amount of work that a CPU can perform is determined by the speed of its internal clock. The faster the clock runs, the more work that the CPU can get done, making for a more powerful computer.

The clock speed of a CPU is measured in megahertz, or MHz, which stands for millions of cycles per second—that's a lot of work. A CPU with a higher clock speed is more powerful than a CPU with a lower clock speed. As you would expect, the more powerful CPUs cost more than the less powerful ones.

(Figure 2.1) The CPU is the "engine" of your computer. Here's a Pentium (left) and a C6x86 (right).

As recently as July of 1996, a typical "starter system" was powered by a 100MHz Pentium-class CPU. However, as we go to press with this book (February 1997), the 100MHz Pentium-class computers are almost unheard of and the 120MHz Pentium-class is now the most common CPU in most

24

starter systems. In Table 2.1 we've listed the street prices of Pentium CPUs as of January 31, 1997. These prices have surely changed since then, but you can see that for a few additional dollars, you get an incremental increase in performance.

Intel CPU	Street price	Intel CPU	Street price
Pentium 75MHz	$ 125	Pentium 133MHz	$ 250
Pentium 90MHz	$ 125	Pentium 150MHz	$ 300
Pentium 100MHz	$ 150	Pentium 166MHz	$ 450
Pentium 120MHz	$ 175	Pentium 200MHz	$ 600

(Table 2.1) Street prices of Pentium CPUs (as of January 1997)

The Cyrix C6x86 CPUs are targeted at users who want better performance at a better price. Cyrix has cleverly named their processors to compete with Intel's Pentiums. For example, the Cyrix C6x86 P120+ runs at an internal clock speed of 100MHz. However, benchmark tests show that the performance of this CPU actually exceeds that of an Intel Pentium 120 CPU. Similarly, the C6x86 P200+ runs at a clock speed of 150MHz yet performs better than an Intel Pentium 200. However, the benchmark tests also show that for heavy floating-point operations, such as for CAD and intensive spreadsheet applications, the Intel Pentiums still command better performance than the Cyrix CPUs.

While there may be some disagreement over which CPU is better, Cyrix does offer an alternative to Intel's Pentiums. C6x86 processors are plug compatible with the Intel Pentium CPU, meaning that the ZIF socket on the motherboard will accommodate either manufacturer's processor.

Cyrix CPU	Clock speed	Street price	Cyrix CPU	Clock speed	Street price
C6x86 P120+	100 MHz	$ 135	C6x86 P166+	133 MHz	$ 225
C6x86 P133+	110 MHz	$ 160	C6x86 P200+	166 MHz	$ 350
C6x86 P150+	120 MHz	$ 175			

(Table 2.2) Street prices of Cyrix C6x86 CPUs (as of January 1997)

Almost all "Pentium" motherboards will accept the C6x86 processors. These motherboards require special jumper settings to handle the different clock speeds and voltage requirements of the Cyrix CPUs. Since they tend to run "hotter" than the Intel processors, make sure that you buy a quality cooling fan that will adequately remove the heat generated by the C6x86 CPUs.

Recently, Intel released a new version of the Pentium called the P55C, more commonly known as MMX. MMX technology is designed to speed up any application that performs repetitive computations on small "chunks" of data in parallel. To support applications such as animations, graphics, video and communications, Intel added 57 new instructions for optimizing these type of operations.

Two models of MMX CPUs are available—one running at 166MHz and the other at 200MHz. Early benchmarks suggest that MMX processors run 10 to 20% faster than a Pentium processor running at the same clock speed. Intel forecasts that these percentages will rise well above half when used with applications designed to take advantage of the new chip's special architecture. However, many familiar with this new hardware say that the speed gain is due mainly to the additional 16K of on-chip cache memory.

At this stage, very few applications can take advantage of the MMX technology. To use these new instructions, existing applications have to be rewritten. It will take many months until the major programs are able to use the new features in the MMX CPUs.

Many of the motherboards that we have used will work with these new MMX CPUs. One way to see if a motherboard does handle them is to look in the motherboard user manual. You'll want to see if there is a reference to the P55C, which is Intel's designation for this CPU.

Since the MMX CPUs are new, you'll pay a premium to buy one of these processors. Volume production is just starting so prices are still high. There is no competitive product to the MMX yet available from Cyrix or AMD.

Go with an MMX CPU only if you need to have the latest. It's still too early to give it the thumbs up.

The bottom line

If you want a better performing PC, buy a faster CPU. However, if you can't afford one of the faster processors today, you can always upgrade to a faster CPU tomorrow. When your budget allows it, you can easily upgrade to a faster processor by simply removing the slower one from the motherboard and inserting the faster CPU and changing a few jumper settings.

In the early months of 1996, CPU prices were falling rapidly. As of January 1997, the prices of CPUs have remained relatively steady. This seems to indicate that CPU prices won't come down appreciably. Our advice is buy that CPU **now**. While it's possible that it may be cheaper tomorrow, you'll also be putting off the utility, fun and pleasure of using your new computer today. *Carpe diem*!!!

CPU COOLING FAN

A Pentium-class CPU has roughly 3 million transistors all jam packed into a package about 2" x 2" (50mm x 50mm) in size. Talk about crowded! All of those busy electrons racing around inside a small ceramic square create a lot of heat.

A Pentium uses about 15 watts of energy. A Cyrix 6x86 uses about 22 watts of energy. This is a lot of heat and both manufacturers recommend that you use a proper cooling fan to remove the heat.

In fact, a fan is so important that most dealers will not sell you a motherboard without a cooling fan. Several reliable sources have told us you should use a specially designed fan with Cyrix CPUs that spin about three times as fast as standard fans in order to cool the chip. These fans also use ball bearings to cut down on wear and tear.

A cooling fan is actually made of two parts: the heat sink and the fan. The heat sink is a square metal plate that sits on top of the Pentium. The fan housing clips over the top of the metal plate and locks the assembly in place. The connectors on the fan are then connected to either a motherboard connector or a power supply connector.

(Figure 2.2) This CPU cooling fan will keep the Pentium running cool.

Do yourself a favor. Don't run a Pentium CPU without a cooling fan.

MOTHERBOARDS

The motherboard is a large circuit board into which the CPU, memory, peripheral cards, various connectors and the supporting circuitry plug.

The motherboard is the most crucial component that you'll have to buy. If you're like other typical users, you'll have more questions about selecting a motherboard than any other component.

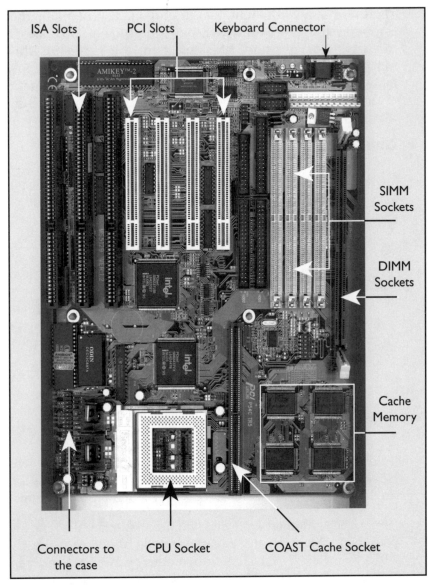

ISA Slots   PCI Slots   Keyboard Connector

SIMM Sockets

DIMM Sockets

Cache Memory

Connectors to the case   CPU Socket   COAST Cache Socket

(Figure 2.3) This is a typical Pentium motherboard. It has three ISA slots, four PCI slots, four 72-pin SIMM sockets, a DIMM socket and a cache socket.

There are many different makes and models of motherboards. In a computer store or at a computer show, you'll likely find dozens of different motherboards for sale. Most of them are made in China, Korea, Malaysia or Taiwan, where the manufacturing costs are low. Since so many companies make motherboards, there's a lot of competition, which means high quality and low prices. As consumers, we benefit from all of this competition.

Choosing a motherboard

In simplest terms, the performance and features provided by any motherboard are determined by which chipset is used on that motherboard. A chipset provides the supporting circuitry to control most of the other components on the motherboard.

For earlier computers, such as 386 models, the control functions were performed by many separate integrated circuits or chips. Each chip controlled a very specific function, such as refreshing the dynamic RAM memory or regulating the high speed DMA transfer to and from a hard drive. But in today's computers, a chipset (usually a set of from two to four highly integrated chips) replaces the numerous separate chips.

There are two main benefits of using chipsets:
1. Motherboards are less prone to problems.
2. Motherboards are less expensive.

In selecting a motherboard, you'll want to consider the following criteria. However, you'll see that your final selection will for the most part be predetermined by which chipset is used on any particular motherboard.

First, select a motherboard that will accommodate the type and speed of your CPU. Most Pentium motherboards also accept the Cyrix C6x86 CPUs. Some inexpensive Pentium motherboards can handle speeds up to 150MHz. Our advice is to buy a motherboard which can handle clock speeds of up to 200MHz. Even if you're not planning to install a 200MHz CPU now, buying a 200MHz motherboard is good insurance for that day when you need the extra horsepower.

For the remainder of this book, when we refer to a Pentium motherboard, what we really mean is a Pentium-class motherboard that also handles Cyrix C6x86 CPUs.

> **NOTE**
>
> To be able to handle the 200MHz Pentium CPUs, the motherboard must have a VRM (Voltage Regulator Module). Some motherboards have built-in VRMs and others have a socket to accept an optional VRM.

Second, select a motherboard that has the type of system bus that you'll be using.

The two choices are the PCI bus and the VL-bus. Practically speaking, no one should select a VL-bus motherboard. In fact, you'll have a hard time finding one to buy.

We only bring this point up because some readers may have VL-bus cards that they'd like to use in their upgraded system. The VL-bus (VESA Local bus) was designed to be used with 486 processors. Plug-in cards for the VL-bus are capable of transferring data to and from the CPU at much higher speeds than the original AT bus, a performance limitation left over from the 286 computers.

Today, almost all Pentium motherboards use the PCI bus. Why? Because Intel has put a lot of effort into making this a standard. Since the PCI bus is capable of transferring data 64 bits at a time at rates up to 75MHz, component manufacturers can make high performance peripherals and add-ons at a low-cost. There are already thousands of PCI add-on cards available.

Some motherboards, called combos, can simultaneously accommodate add-on cards for both the PCI bus and VL-bus. If you absolutely need to use both types of cards in your PC, you can choose one of these combo motherboards. Otherwise, go with the PCI bus.

In addition to PCI bus slots and/or VL-bus slots, all motherboards also have slots for older ISA or EISA plug-in cards as well. This lets you use the "legacy" 8-bit and 16-bit ISA cards and 32-bit EISA cards in your new PC. A typical Pentium motherboard has three or four slots for PCI or VL-bus cards and three or four slots for ISA/EISA cards.

Since the PCI bus is now a *de facto* standard for Pentium systems, make it your choice too.

Third, select a motherboard based on whether or not you want onboard I/O. A motherboard with onboard I/O has the built-in electronics for controlling four fixed drives, two floppy drives, two communication ports, a parallel port and usually a game port. Buying a motherboard with onboard I/O means that you won't have to buy a separate add-on board for handling the I/O.

Onboard I/O also frees up one of the slots on the motherboard, a factor worth considering if your case is small or you are planning to add a lot of peripheral cards. Make sure that the onboard I/O has these characteristics: EIDE (Enhanced IDE) interface capable of handling 4 fixed drives and 2 floppy drives, one parallel and two high speed serial communications ports using 16550 UARTs for faster, more reliable data transfer.

Fourth, select a motherboard which supports *pipeline burst cache*. Caching is a way to speed up access to main memory. Using standard cache, four bytes of data can be transferred from cache to the CPU in eight clock cycles. A special feature of the Pentiums is its ability to access memory in *burst* mode where the same four bytes of data can be transferred in only five clock cycles. On some motherboards the cache is already built-in. On other motherboards, the cache is added separately. The more recent motherboards accept a type of cache called COAST memory. COAST is an acronym for Cache On A STick—a clever name for the small circuit boards which accommodate the pipeline burst cache memory.

Fifth, select a motherboard which supports the type and amount of memory that you're likely to use. Most Pentium motherboards have four sockets which accept 72-pin SIMMs. Since a single 72-pin SIMM has a from 4MB to 32MB, a motherboard with four sockets can have from 8MB (using two 4MB SIMMs) to 128MB (using four 32MB SIMMs). If you need more memory, look for a motherboard that has six or more 72-pin SIMM sockets.

Some motherboards also have sockets that accept the older 30-pin SIMMs. If you're on a tight budget and have a considerable amount of money invested in 30-pin SIMMs, then you can extend your investment in this older memory by selecting a motherboard that has sockets for both 30-pin memory and 72-pin memory. Otherwise, we recommend buying a motherboard that accommodates only 72-pin SIMMs.

Most of the Pentium motherboards are able to take advantage of the faster EDO memory. EDO SIMMs are 10-15% faster than non-EDO memory, but the faster access time is available only on motherboards specially designed to use EDO SIMMs. You should select one of these motherboards even if you aren't initially planning to use EDO memory.

Many users prefer to buy non-parity memory. If you are one of those who like the security which parity memory offers, make sure that the motherboard supports parity checking. Turn to the Memory section of this chapter for more information on parity.

Chipsets

Next are a few of the major chipsets used on Pentium motherboards. When you're selecting a motherboard, you can determine which features the motherboard supports based on which chipset is used on that motherboard.

Acer Labs Aladdin chipset

- ❖ PCI bus only with ISA support

- ❖ I/O onboard

- ❖ Keyboard controller

- ❖ Up to 1MB of write-back pipeline burst cache

- ❖ Parity and non-parity memory up to 768MB; supports EDO memory

Intel Triton FX chipset

- ❖ PCI bus with ISA support

- ❖ I/O onboard for up to 4 IDE devices

- ❖ Pipeline burst cache

- ❖ Non-parity only memory up to 128MB; supports EDO memory

- ❖ Power management

Intel Triton II HX chipset

- ❖ PCI bus with ISA support

- ❖ I/O onboard for up to 4 IDE drives

- ❖ Pipeline burst cache

- ❖ Parity and non-parity memory up to 512MB; supports EDO memory

- ❖ Power management

- ❖ Universal Serial Bus support

Intel Triton III VX chipset

- ❖ PCI bus with ISA support

- ❖ I/O onboard for up to 4 IDE drives

- ❖ Pipeline burst cache

- ❖ Memory access about 10%-15% faster than Triton FX chipset

- ❖ Parity and non-parity memory up to 512MB; supports EDO memory; supports synchronous DRAM

- ❖ Power management

- ❖ Universal Serial Bus support

Opti Viper chipset

- ❖ PCI bus and VL bus with ISA support

- ❖ I/O onboard

- ❖ Up to 2MB of write-back pipeline burst cache

- ❖ Parity and non-parity memory to 512MB; supports EDO memory

SIS chipset

- ❖ PCI bus and VL bus

- ❖ I/O onboard for up to 4 IDE devices

- ❖ Pipeline burst cache

- ❖ 2MB of write-back cache

- ❖ Parity and non-parity memory up to 512MB; supports EDO memory

- ❖ Power management

35

OTHER CONSIDERATIONS

Selecting a motherboard based on its chipset eliminates many of the decisions that we have to make in selecting a motherboard. However, here's several other things to consider:

Select a motherboard that has a BIOS from one of the major manufacturers. The BIOS is a small chip which contains the most important program instructions for initializing and testing the computer at startup, setting the Plug-'n'-Play devices and handling the computer's basic functions for inputting and outputting data, for example. We recommend a motherboard which has a Plug-'n'-Play *Flash BIOS*. A flash BIOS is made using a chip that is reprogrammable, meaning that the functions can be easily updated at a later time using a program supplied by the manufacturer. The program is usually supplied on a diskette when you buy the motherboard. The major BIOS manufacturers are AMI (American Megatrends International), Award, DTK, Microid Research and Phoenix.

Plug-'n'- Play

This is a recent innovation whose goal is to automate the configuration of new peripherals in a computer system. When the BIOS and operating system recognize a new Plug-'n'-Play peripheral, it can automatically decide how to configure the IRQs, DMAs, and other technical specifications. Plug-'n'-Play requires that the BIOS, operating system and peripheral device all meet the Plug-'n'-Play specifications.

Select a motherboard that has a built-in mouse port. Without a mouse port, adding a mouse to your computer system requires you to use one of the computer's two serial ports or buy a separate add-on card for the mouse.

Select the motherboard based on its layout. Some motherboards have better physical configurations than others. For example, we've found motherboards that are unable to accept a full-length add-on card because it won't fit into the slot without interfering with one or more other components on the motherboard. Check the layout to assure yourself that this won't be a problem.

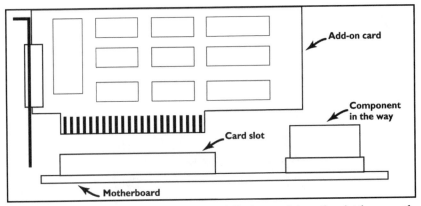

(Figure 2.4) This add-in card cannot be fully inserted into the slot because the component already on the motherboard is in the way.

To make their products more attractive, some manufacturers have added other features to their motherboards:

❖ Built-in video display card

❖ Built-in sound card

❖ Built-in SCSI I/O adapter

In order to build a flexible system, we recommend that you select a motherboard that does not have any of these additional features. While the price of a motherboard with a built-in video display card or sound card may be attractive, you loose the some of the flexibility for future upgrades. Instead, we recommend separate plug-in cards that perform each of these particular functions. By taking this approach, you'll build a system that can be easily upgraded at a later time.

NOTE

Don't buy a motherboard without the user's manual. The user's manual has very specific and necessary instructions for setting the various jumpers and switches. Configuring your motherboard is one of the most critical steps in building a trouble-free PC and the user's manual is a required component.

MEMORY

We assume that your present 486 system already has 72-pin SIMMs that you'll be able to use in your upgraded system. We talk a little about memory here so that you'll have additional information for when you're interested in adding more memory at a later time.

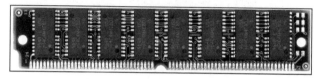

(Figure 2.5) A 72-pin SIMM

A computer's main memory, or RAM, is built from small circuit boards called SIMMs. Pentium motherboards are designed to use standard 72-pin SIMMs. If you count the "fingers" on the bottom edge of a SIMM, you'll know why it is called a 72-pin module.

Most Pentium motherboards have four 72-pin sockets. The four sockets are organized as two banks of two sockets each. These are identified as Bank 0 and Bank 1. You can see the two banks in Figure 2.6. By design, both sockets in a bank must contain SIMMs; therefore, you have to add SIMMs to the motherboard in pairs; you cannot add a single SIMM at a time. Bank 0 must be filled before Bank 1. For a 16MB system, you can use two 8MB SIMMs in Bank 0 or four 4MB SIMMs in both Bank 0 and Bank 1.

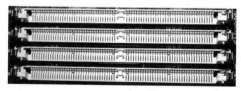

(Figure 2.6) This motherboard has four 72-pin SIMM sockets.

When you're buying memory, you may see it advertised with a lot of technical numbers. Here's an example of an advertisement for memory:

38

4MB 1x32 70ns 72-pin SIMMs	$30
8MB 2x32 60ns 72-pin SIMMs w/EDO	$60
16MB 4x36 70ns 72-pin SIMMs w/parity	$125
32MB 8x32 60ns 72-pin SIMMs	$240

(Figure 2.7) Here's a sample of how you might see memory advertised.

To help you understand what this all means, let's decode some of this jargon. When you select RAM, you have to specify several characteristics:

Amount of memory on the SIMM—this represents the amount of RAM that the module adds to your computer. The amount is stated in MB (for millions of bytes).

Arrangement of chips on the SIMM—this describes the way in which the individual chips are accessed on the SIMM. For our purposes, you can consider this value to be another way of describing the amount of memory on the SIMM as shown on the right.

Arrangement	Capacity
1X32 or 1X36	4MB
2X32 or 2X36	8MB
4X32 or 4X36	16MB
8X32 or 8X36	32MB

Time to access data

This represents the amount of time required to access any piece of data within the SIMM. The time is represented in ns (for *nanoseconds*—which is one-billionth of a second!!). In the above examples, the 4MB SIMM has a speed of 70 nanoseconds while the 8MB SIMM has a 60 nanosecond speed. For Pentiums 120MHz and above, use 60-nanosecond SIMMs or faster. You can mix two SIMMs of different speeds, for example 70ns and 60ns SIMMs. However, the access speed will be the slower of the pair, 60ns in this case.

Parity or non-parity

This determines whether a SIMM has parity checking. Parity checking is a way to make a computer's memory more reliable. Without parity checking a byte of RAM is composed of 8 bits of memory; with parity checking a byte of RAM is made up of 9 bits of memory. The extra bit is a "check" bit, which is used to make sure that the data in the remaining 8 bits is valid. If you see the designation 1x36 or 2x36 or 4x36 or 8x36, then you'll know that this is a SIMM with parity bits.

> **NOTE**
>
> Many Pentium motherboards sold today use non-parity SIMMs. Make sure that the memory you buy matches the type of memory supported by the motherboard. If you are building a PC which absolutely requires the utmost in up-time and data security, choose a motherboard that use parity memory.

EDO or non-EDO

EDO stands for **E**xtended **D**ata **O**ut and is a newer type of SIMM that is 10 to 15 percent faster than conventional SIMMs. An EDO SIMM fits in all motherboards that accept 72-pin SIMMs, but the faster access time is available only if the motherboard is designed specifically to use EDO SIMMs.

Always buy SIMMs in pairs. Most memory specialists recommend that both SIMMs in a pair are made by the same manufacturer. For the small difference in price between EDO and non-EDO SIMMs, we recommend that you go with the EDO type and enjoy the performance gain.

The bottom line

Don't upgrade your system with less than 16MB of memory. It's not very economical to upgrade to a fast Pentium processor only to squander its power with less memory, especially if you're later planning to run Windows 95. Sure you can try to run with a small amount of memory, but you won't be happy with an under-performing PC.

CACHE MEMORY

There isn't much to selecting cache memory. When you're selecting your motherboard, the salesman will most likely ask you if you also want to add cache memory. Depending on the design of the motherboard, you'll want to add one of two types of cache memory: static RAM chips or COAST modules (some motherboards such as ours have onboard cache built-in, but also let us upgrade to more cache memory by adding a COAST module).

Figure 2.8 shows a single SRAM chip. SRAM is the abbreviation for Static RAM. These chips come in different capacities. If your motherboard has 8 sockets totaling 256K, you'll want to buy eight 32K x 8 SRAM chips, which costs roughly $40. Here's some ballpark prices for SRAM:

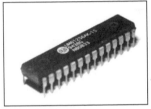

(Figure 2.8) Static RAM cache

32K X 8 SRAM	$5.00 each
64K X 8 SRAM	$8.50 each
128K X 8 SRAM	$16.00 each

A second type of add-on cache is supplied as a COAST module, as we see in Figure 2.9. This module easily plugs into a special socket on the motherboard. If your motherboard has a slot for a COAST cache module, you'll be able to buy a 256K module for about $40.

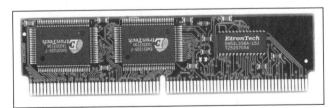

(Figure 2.9) A COAST module

Cache memory is very fast, with cycle times of about 15 nanoseconds. By adding cache to your system, you can enhance the performance of your computer system for a very nominal cost.

The bottom line

Cache memory is a good investment for insuring that your upgraded system will run at top performance.

VIDEO DISPLAY CARDS

Selecting a good video display card is critical to making your PC perform well. Pentiums are so powerful and the amount of data that these CPUs can process is considerable. Most of you will use either Windows 3.11 or Window 95. These graphical interfaces "draw" tremendous amounts of text to the screen by way of the video display card. Thus a slow video display card can *waste* the speed of a fast Pentium CPU.

Earlier PCs were designed around the classic 16-bit ISA (Industry Standard Association) bus or the later 32-bit EISA (Extended ISA) bus. This limited pathway to the video card was therefore a bottleneck to fast video performance. If you're thinking about using an older ISA-bus video display card, **DON'T**. Today's newer video display cards offer a tremendous performance gain over the ISA video display cards. Don't upgrade your CPU without upgrading its video.

The PCI bus and VL-bus were designed to improve the video performance of ISA systems by moving data between the CPU and the video display card at a much faster speed. Today, both the PCI and VLB system bus on a Pentium motherboard provide a wider, streamlined pathway for the video data, which greatly improves the overall PC performance. Don't try to save money by reusing your older generation video display card. Instead, buy a PCI (or VLB, as a last resort) video display card, making sure it matches the system bus of your motherboard.

When selecting a video display card, you usually have to select the type and amount of memory for the card. These two factors determine the display speed and maximum display resolution of the card. There are two types of memory—DRAM and VRAM. DRAM (**D**ynamic **RAM**) is the same type of memory as the computer system's main memory. A card with DRAM is less expensive than the same card with VRAM. A video display card with VRAM (**V**ideo **RAM**) can generate the display faster. VRAM is "dual-ported"—there are two paths to the same memory location. This second path lets the video circuitry access the VRAM at the same time as the CPU, so that neither one has to wait for the other.

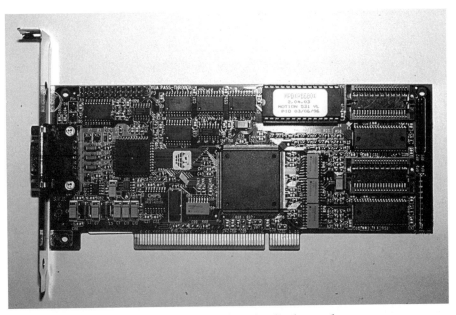

(Figure 2.10) A PCI video display card

A video display card with more memory can operate at a higher resolution. If you're planning to run mostly word processing or accounting applications on your PC, then 1MB of video memory is probably sufficient. But for more highly graphical applications, such as CAD, games or desktop publishing, you may want to consider a card with 2MB of video memory. Keep in mind that the maximum resolution of the card can be achieved only if your monitor is capable of displaying that resolution. At a later point in time, you can upgrade a 1MB DRAM video card for about $40-$50 to gain higher resolution and color depth.

ATI, Cirrus Logic, Diamond, Genoa, Hercules, Matrox, Number Nine, Orchid and Trident are well-known manufacturers of video display cards.

The bottom line

A PCI video card will do wonders to improve the performance of a Pentium system. DRAM is fast enough for most applications, but for intensive graphics and CAD work, you should consider VRAM.

First Things First

Chapter 3

First Things First

Before we jump into this head first, we have to take a few precautions.

Don't take the following steps lightly. It takes only a few minutes to perform these steps (compared to the hours (upon hours) you'll spend rebuilding if the worst should happen). When they're complete, you rest more securely knowing that you have protected your system.

Step 1 — Back Up Your Hard Disk(s)

Yes, it is possible to upgrade a computer without taking a backup of your hard drive. And no, we don't expect to have any problems with the hard drive since we're not going to be upgrading the operating system or any of the applications during this operation. However, unforeseen things can occur. Having a backup of your hard drive is one of the best ways of insuring that the operation is a success.

It's easy to backup your hard drive(s) if you already have a tape backup drive or another mass storage backup unit, such as a Zip drive or EZ-Drive. If not, you can backup the data onto a set of floppy disks. Backing up to floppies isn't a pleasant chore, but it's even more unpleasant to lose your valuable data, applications and the time required to put things back in order should you lose your hard drive.

Step 2	Save Your Current Configuration

If you're using DOS or Windows 3.11, run Microsoft's MSD diagnostics. This gives you a snapshot of the settings for your fully functioning 486 computer system. This information contains IRQ, DMA and memory configuration information that may be valuable after you complete the upgrade.

Run MSD from DOS, not from Windows 3.11.

From the main menu, select **File** | **Print Report**. Then select **Report All** and type "486SYS.MSD" under **File:**. This creates a file on your hard disk containing the entire MSD report. Copy this file from your hard disk to a floppy and store the floppy in a safe place. In this example, file 486SYS.MSD has the complete configuration information for our original 486 computer system.

(Figure 3.1) The MSD Report Screen

If you're running Windows 95 you can obtain the system configuration information by starting at the **Control Panel** folder. Double-click the **System** icon. Next select the **Device Manager** tab. Now click on **Print**. For **Report type**, select the **All devices and system summary** button, the **Print**

to file check box and finally the **OK** button. The file dialog box will open and you can type "486SYS.PRN" as the file name. Again, the report file is written to the hard disk and you can copy the file to a floppy for safekeeping.

The most useful settings are the current IRQs, DMAs and I/O port addresses that the system is using. In addition to the complete reports from above, it is helpful to print the IRQ settings, DMA addresses and I/O port addresses using either MSD for your DOS/Windows 3.x system or via the System icon for your Windows 95 system. Keep these in a handy place in case you need to refer to them later during the upgrade.

Step 3 | Copy Your BIOS Settings

This step is not as straight-forward as Step 2 because the BIOS information is presented in varying formats by the different setup programs.

Although your new Pentium motherboard will have a very smart BIOS, later you may need to enter information about your hard drive. The key information that you should record for each hard drive in your original system are:

- ❖ Number of cylinders
- ❖ Number of heads
- ❖ Number of sectors per track

If you don't already know these parameters, you can view them by using the BIOS setup program. To start the BIOS setup program, consult your manual. If you can't find the correct key sequence, try pressing these as your system is first starting up (see the following table).

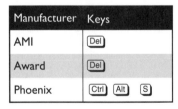

Manufacturer	Keys
AMI	Del
Award	Del
Phoenix	Ctrl Alt S

Your BIOS settings will look something like this:

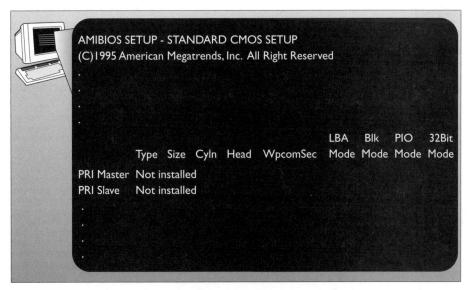

(Figure 3.2) Hard drive settings from the BIOS

3

Step 4	Prepare Your Work Area

Not many of us are big fans of house work. But sometimes, we just have to force ourselves to clean house, which in turn makes our lives a little more orderly.

It's easier said than done, but make the effort to clear a flat, open work area about six by four feet so that you can upgrade your system without falling all over yourself.

An oversized card table, a workbench or a desk works well. The work surface should be clean. If the work surface cannot be washed, spread clean, white paper over the area. Don't use newspaper because it's hard to find small parts when they drop onto news articles or pictures.

The work area should be well lighted. Since the inside of a computer is usually dark, any extra light will make the upgrade easier. Avoid drafty areas since small parts are likely to be blown away and lost.

(Figure 3.3) A clean, well-lighted area will make your upgrade go smoother.

Gather Your Tools

You don't need very many tools to upgrade your computer. Here's what we used for our upgrade:

- ❖ Phillips-head screwdriver, #1 head

- ❖ flat-head screwdriver with 1/8" blade

- ❖ 3/8" nutdriver

- ❖ Long-nose pliers

- ❖ Several small paper cups (e.g., bathroom Dixie cups) for holding small screws and parts

- ❖ Large mouse pad or small hand towel on which to place the motherboard

- ❖ Pen and pad of paper to take notes

(Figure 3.4) These are all the tools we need to upgrade a 486.

If the only Phillips-head screwdriver you own is too big or too small, then STOP. Go to a hardware store and buy one of the correct size. You risk damaging the components or stripping the screw heads by using the wrong tool. A new tool costs only a few dollars. Compare this small expense to the amount of money you're investing in your upgrade.

Disassembling
Your 486

Chapter 4

Disassembling Your 486

Most readers have already had their computers apart and may be quite familiar with many of the steps which we'll describe here. If you've already operated on your 486 before, then you may not need to follow all of the details in each of these steps. However, you might do well to read through this chapter to make sure that you haven't missed anything important.

We've followed these same steps many, many times as we have successfully upgraded many 486 systems. We won't claim that we know the absolute best way to upgrade a 486, but we can say that this way works for us.

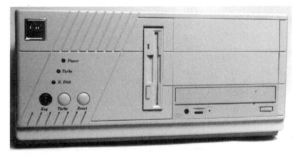

(Figure 4.1) A typical 486 in a desktop case

(Figure 4.2) A typical 486 in a mini-tower case

There are many hundreds of styles of 486 computers. With so many variations, it's not possible to have photos or illustrations for each style. For this practical reason, we've chosen to upgrade a "typical" 486 whose case and insides are commonly sold by computer retailers, discounters and superstores. You won't have any trouble recognizing the equivalent components or parts in your 486.

Step 1 | Detach The External Cables From Your Computer

Make sure that the power to your computer is turned off! You'd be surprised to know that on several occasions we forgot to turn the power off. It's not a mistake one makes twice. Whenever you're working inside the computer, it's a good idea to not only turn the power off, but also unplug the power cord from the wall. **Take this precaution seriously**.

Besides the power cord, you'll want to detach the various wires and cables plugged into the back of your computer system. Unplug the following:

❖ Keyboard connector

❖ Monitor connector

❖ Mouse connector—be sure to note the serial port to which the mouse was connected — either COM1 or COM2. You'll need to know this when you reinstall the mouse later.

❖ Network cable—coax or RJ-45—if your computer system is connected to a network

❖ Telephone line cord—if your computer system has a modem

Now your computer should be free of *wire clutter*.

(Figure 4.3) Here's the cable clutter on our computer

Step 2	Remove The Cover

Place your computer on a clean, well-lighted work surface. Next determine if your case is a screwless.

Some cases are *screwless*—you can remove the cover from the case without having to use a screwdriver. If your case is of this variety, look at the owner's manual to find out how to open it. Figure 4.4 shows a 486 system whose case pops open without a screwdriver.

First, you snap the front panel off. Then the hood slides back a few inches and lifts off.

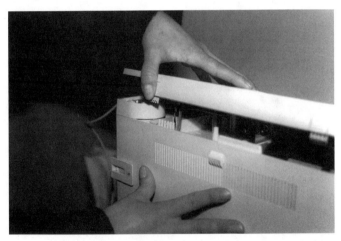

(Figure 4.4) This is a screwless case. After popping off the front panel, the rest of the case slides off to expose the insides of the computer.

Other covers are attached to the case with screws. The screws are found on the back of the case. Turn the case around so that the back of the case is facing you. Usually, five or six hex-head screws are used to secure the case cover to the frame. Unscrew these and place them in one of the small paper cups. Label the cup so that you'll know where the screws came from. Set the cover aside and away from the work area for now.

(Figure 4.5) Four hex head screws (circled in this photo) hold the cover onto this case.

After the cover is removed, position the case frame with the back of the computer facing toward you on your work surface.

If you have a tower-style case, lay the computer horizontally with the motherboard chassis closest to the work surface, as in Figure 4.6.

(Figure 4.6) If you have a tower chassis, position it horizontally.

We're almost ready to operate.

Step 3	Discharge Electrostatic Energy

What we used to call static electricity, is now referred to as "electrostatic energy." By either name it can damage delicate components. To prevent any damage, discharge this energy from yourself before handling the components.

A simple way to do this is to ground yourself. When your computer is plugged into a three-prong wall outlet, your computer case is grounded. **You do not have to turn on the power to the computer** in order to ground the case.

To discharge yourself of electrostatic energy, touch the metal computer case. After you've discharged yourself, **unplug the power cord**.

Another way to discharge the electrostatic energy is to wear a specially designed wrist strap (see Figure 4.7). This device looks like a wrist watch that is attached to a dog's leash. The leash is connected to a ground and the other end wraps around your wrist. By wearing the wrist strap, you're always grounded.

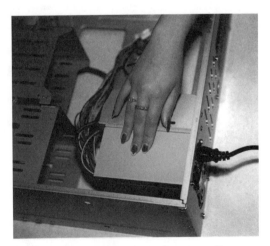

(Figure 4.7) Discharge electrostatic energy by grounding yourself to the case.

63

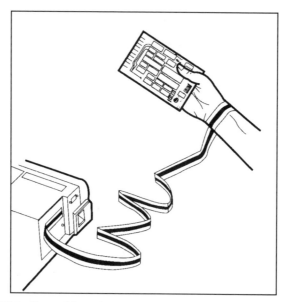

(Figure 4.8) This disposable wrist strap can be used to avoid electrostatic energy damage to delicate electronic components.

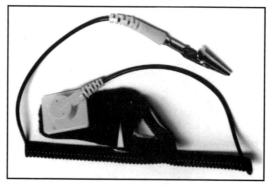

(Figure 4.9) This reusable wriststrap clips to a ground.

If you're interested in purchasing a grounding wrist strap, check out these two brands:

❖ 3M Disposable Grounding Wrist Strap, part # 2209

❖ Charleswater Adjustable Wrist Strap w/6' coiled cord, part # 14810

Both are available from:

Marshall Industries
9320 Telstar Ave
El Monte, CA 91731
Phone (800) 432-2222 Fax (818) 307-6173
www.marshall.com

Step 4 | Remove Add-on Cards

Most users have several add-on cards in their computer. You're probably aware of how "messy" the insides of the computer can be, especially before your remove these cards.

Even though you may have only a few cards, it's easy to lose track of their purposes when you remove them from the case. Therefore we recommend that you remove them in an orderly manner. When you remove a card, carefully place it on a soft terrycloth towel.

The order in which you remove the cards is important only from the point of view of mechanics. I usually remove the cards with cables that are "in the way" first. By removing these, it's easier to access the other cards that may be suffering from cable strangulation.

(Figure 4.10) These four cards have to be removed before we can reach the motherboard.

There isn't any *right* way to remove a card, but here are a few tips.

❖ Unscrew the small screw holding the add-on card to the back panel.

❖ Detach any cables that are connected to the card.

❖ Remove the card by gently rocking it back and forth in its slot. Rock the card only a few millimeters in each direction. Do not use force or you risk damaging the card or another one in an adjacent slot.

❖ After you remove the card, carefully place it on a soft surface together with any cables that you have detached.

❖ Note the type of card which you removed, e.g., sound card, modem, etc.

After you have removed one card from the chassis, move on to the next.

In our example, we removed the following cards:

❖ Sound card with CD-ROM controller

❖ VGA video display card

❖ I/O card

❖ Ethernet network card

Step 5 | Unplug Cables From Hard Drive And Floppy Drive

Your 486 may have a hard and floppy drive controller built into the motherboard or a separate I/O card which also handles the serial, parallel and game ports.

If you have a separate I/O card, you have already removed the card and the cables in the previous step.

If you have a built-in hard and floppy drive controller, you should now remove the cables from the motherboard which connect to your hard drive(s) and floppy drive(s). The ends of these cables simply unplug from each component.

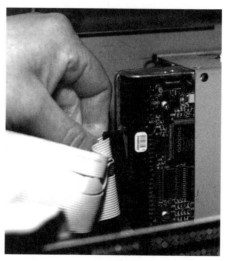

(Figure 4.11) Removing the hard drive and floppy drive cables.

Step 6	Remove Drive Cage

A drive cage accommodates 3.5" storage devices. A cage lets you easily install these devices to your computer system and conversely uninstall these devices. In our case, we have one hard drive and one floppy drive mounted in a removable drive cage.

(Figure 4.12) Removing the drive cage lets you get the motherboard out more easily.

This cage is secured to the case by a single screw. After we unscrew it, the cage slides towards the back of the case for easily removal.

Step 7 | Remove The Power Supply

Most computer systems are built compactly to save space on your desktop. One of the largest components in the computer is the power supply, which is one of the factors determining the size of the case.

Because the power supply is so large, if we remove it from the case, we'll be able to more easily work on the motherboard. The power supply in this case is mounted directly above two connectors to the motherboard. To detach these two connectors from the motherboard, we have to first remove the power supply.

(Figure 4.13) Four hex head screws hold the power supply to the case.

Make sure that the power cord has been unplugged from the wall socket before you remove the power supply from your case. This power supply is attached to the case with four hex head screws. When these are unscrewed, you can lift the power supply out of the case, as in Figure 4.14.

(Figure 4.14) With the screws removed, you can lift the power supply from the case.

The two connectors from the power supply to the motherboard are still attached. Each connector has six wires. The connectors are usually labeled P8 and P9. These two sets of wires supply power to the motherboard.

Remove the two P8 and P9 connectors as in Figure 4.15. These may be fastened quite securely to the motherboard. One side of the connector may have a small plastic tab that locks it in place. Using a small bladed screwdriver, gently pry the plastic tab away from the motherboard connector as you are pulling on the wires.

(Figure 4.15) Removing the P8 and P9 power supply connectors from the motherboard.

An electrical cord runs from the power supply to the on/off switch on the rear panel of the case. If the cord is long enough to sit adjacent to the case, you won't have to detach it. If you find that you have to detach the cord (ours has four connectors) from the on/off switch, carefully note the orientation of the wires so that you can later reinstall the connectors correctly (see Figure 4.16 on the right).

(Figure 4.16) These four wires run from the power supply to the on/off switch. If you remove them, carefully note the color of each so you can properly reinstall them later.

Step 8   Detach Other Case Wires

By now, your 486 will be looking kind of empty. We have a few more details to wrap up yet.

There are various switches, buttons and lights on the case that are used by the computer. These are connected to the motherboard by different sets of wires, as in Figure 4.17.

So that you'll be able to identify the purpose of each set of wires, you'll have to take notes. As you disconnect a set of wires from the old 486 motherboard, you'll want to note the colors of the wires (e.g., red/white pair) and the corresponding connector (e.g., HDD Led) to which it is attached. A label indicating the purpose of a connector is usually etched onto the motherboard next to the small pins to which the connector attaches.

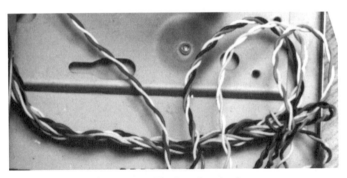

(Figure 4.17) Spaghetti wires

The following table is an example of the wires that were used in one of the 486es that we recently upgraded:

Wire Sets	Features	Wire Sets	Features
Red/White	HDD Led	Yellow/White	Turbo Led
Green/White	Power Led	Blue/White	Reset switch
Black/Orange	Keylock	Orange/White/Blac	Turbo switch
Red/Black	Speaker		

(Table 4-1) Wire set connections

Of course, your notes will probably list different colors. However, most 486es will have the same features we've listed in the table.

Step 9	Remove The Motherboard

We're now ready for the last step—removing the 486 motherboard.

A motherboard is held in place by a combination of screws and plastic fasteners called "standoffs." There are usually five to eight screws and/or standoffs holding it in place.

Locate the screws which secure the motherboard to the case.

(Figure 4-18) This 486 motherboard is attached to the case with two screws and six plastic standoffs.

You'll also see the tops of the plastic standoffs peeping up through the motherboard. Usually, a standoff is attached to the case in a channel. With the screws removed, you'll be able to slide the motherboard towards the wide end of the channel—only an inch, but enough to clear the narrow end of the channel, as in Figure 4-19. You can then lift the motherboard from the case.

75

(Figure 4-19) The standoffs hold the motherboard to the case when they are at the narrow end of the channel.

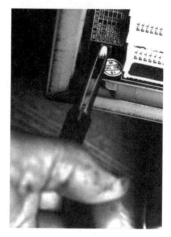

(Figure 4-20) Squeeze the umbrella-like lock on the standoff so that you can detach the motherboard.

If you're not able to slide the standoffs, then you'll have to detach the motherboard from the standoffs. Using a pair of long-nose pliers, gently squeeze the top of the standoff as in Figure 4.20. As you squeeze the standoff, you are compressing the umbrella-like lock which allows you to slide the standoff apart from the motherboard. When you have detached all of the standoffs, you'll be able to remove the motherboard from the inside of the case.

Now you'll have an empty case with a lot of wires hanging out of it, as in Figure 4.21.

(Figure 4.21)   With the motherboard removed, we can clean the insides before installing the new Pentium system.

If you're like me, you won't want to do this next step. Clean the inside of the empty case. It will only take two minutes. You should wipe the dust, dirt and paper particles from the inside of the case with a damp cloth or paper towel. It's amazing how much junk can build up inside an enclosed appliance.

The Upgrade

Chapter 5

The Upgrade

Step 1	Configure The Motherboard

In this step, you'll *configure*, or set up, the motherboard. Here's where you'll have to **carefully read the user's manual** for your motherboard. In the user's manual, find the instructions for setting any *DIP switches* and/or *jumpers* for the motherboard. Here are a few basics that should be helpful.

DIP switches are usually a collection of two to eight miniature light switches on a small plastic base soldered to the motherboard. The individual switches are numbered and the label on the base indicates whether a given switch is on or off. To turn a switch on, use a ball-point pen or small screwdriver to move the switch in the **ON** direction. To turn a switch off, move the switch **opposite** the **ON** direction. Here's a typical row of DIP switches on a motherboard:

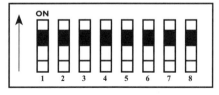

(Figure 5.1) This is a typical DIP switch assembly. This assembly has eight separate switches.

A *jumper* is another kind of switch. You'll notice that there are several metal pins sticking up from the surface of the motherboard. The pins may be labeled JP1 or J10, for examples. A jumper cap is a small metal connector surrounded by insulated plastic (most jumper caps are black in color). When you put the jumper cap on two of the pins, you *close* or *turn on* the switch. If you don't put a jumper cap on the pins, then the switch is said to be *open* or *turned off*. In some cases the pins on the motherboard are paired and labeled 1 and 2; in other cases, there may be three pins labeled 1, 2 and 3. You may be asked to select one option by jumpering pins 1 and 2 or other option by jumpering pins 2 and 3.

For example, in Figure 5.2 the setting is made by jumpering pins 2 and 3.

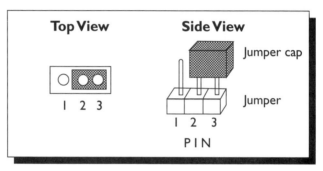

(Figure 5.2) The top view tells us that we should jumper pins 2 and 3. The side view illustrates how to place the jumper cap over these two pins.

In this book we also refer to *connectors*.

In one instance, a *connector* may refer to a set of pins on the motherboard (usually from 2 to 40 pins), as in Figure 5.3.

(Figure 5.3) The connectors are on this motherboard are located beneath the SIMM sockets.

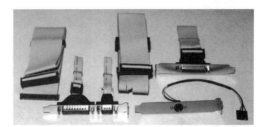

(Figure 5.4) These connectors are all on cables

A *connector* may also refer to the plastic plug (usually black in color) at the end of a set of wires or cable which is attached to the pins. Figure 5.4 shows a variety of connectors.

Now onto the motherboard. The motherboard in Figure 5.5 is a typical Pentium-class motherboard.

(Figure 5.5) This Pentium-class motherboard has three ISA slots, four PCI slots and sockets for up to four 72-pin SIMMs.

Figure 5.6 is a schematic of the motherboard in Figure 5.5. The schematic indicates the location of the important parts of the motherboard. The labels refer to the built-in chips, slots, jumpers and connectors. The key to the abbreviations are identified in the motherboard's user's manual.

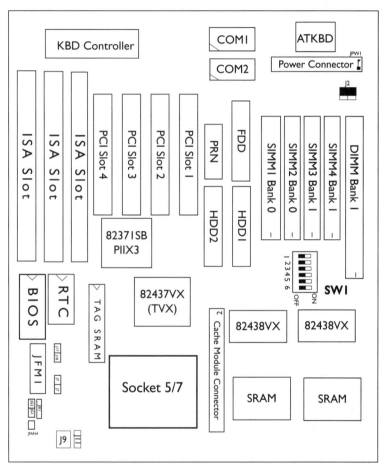

Figure 5.6   Schematic of the motherboard in Figure 5.5

Before handling your motherboard, you'll be wise to rid yourself of electrostatic energy as we explained in Chapter 4.

To protect the motherboard, place it on a soft, padded surface. A large mouse pad is an ideal surface protector. You can also use a hand towel or a few paper towels. Our motherboard was packed with a white foam pad which is good for preventing any damage to the motherboard and to the work surface (the bottom of the motherboard has sharp edges).

In general, configuring the motherboard involves the following:

❖ Specifying the CPU speed

❖ Specifying the CPU voltage

CPU speed

The settings for CPU speed are usually straightforward. Below are the DIP switch settings that specify the CPU speed for our particular motherboard.

Settings for Cyrix 6x86 CPUs	
CPU Speed	SWI Settings
P120+ (100 MHZ)	1 2 3 4 5 6 — On Off
P133+ (110 MHZ)	1 2 3 4 5 6 — On Off
P150+ (120 MHZ)	1 2 3 4 5 6 — On Off
P166+ (133 MHZ)	1 2 3 4 5 6 — On Off

(Figure 5.7) CPU speed settings for Cyrix processors for our motherboard (taken from user's manual)

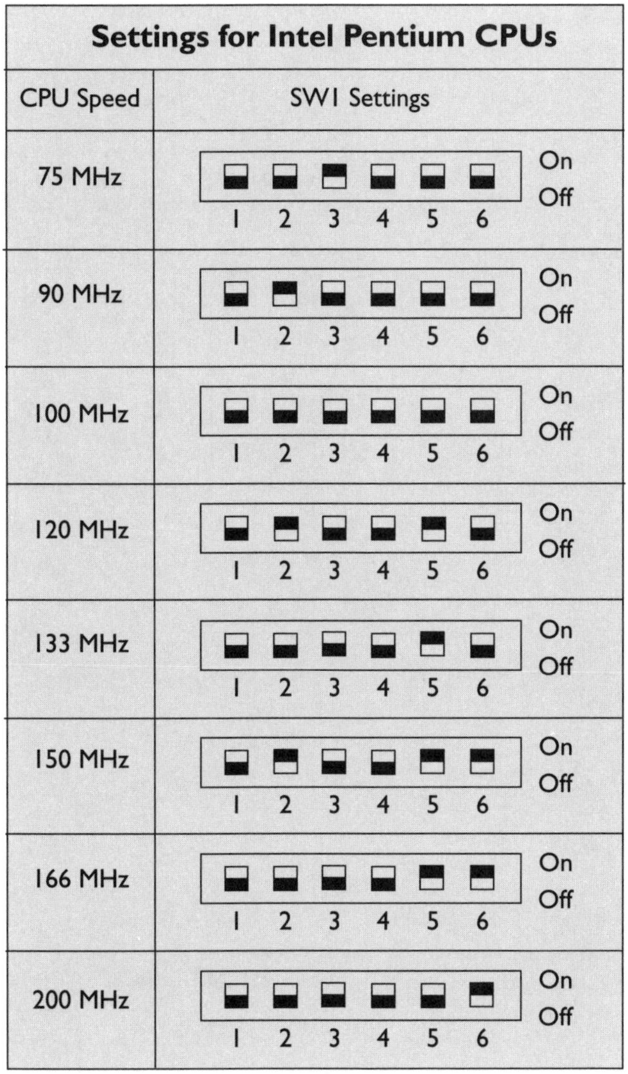
Settings for Intel Pentium CPUs
CPU Speed
SW1 Settings
75 MHz
90 MHz
100 MHz
120 MHz
133 MHz
150 MHz
166 MHz
200 MHz
1 2 3 4 5 6
On
Off

(Figure 5.8) CPU speed settings for Intel processors for our motherboard (taken from user's manual)

Settings for AMD 5k86 CPUs	
CPU Speed	SW1 Settings
P75 (75 MHZ)	
P90 (90 MHZ)	
P100+ (100 MHZ)	

(Figure 5.9) CPU speed settings for AMD processors for our motherboard (taken from user's manual)

The diagrams in Figure 5.7 through Figure 5.9 are from the user's guide for the motherboard pictured in Figure 5.5. You can see in the middle diagram that to configure the motherboard for a Cyrix P-150+ CPU, you'd set SW1 DIP switches 2 and 5 to **on**. To find the location of SW1, see the schematic in Figure 5.6. For equivalent settings, you'll have to consult the user's manual for your motherboard..

CPU voltage

The settings for CPU voltage are also quite easy to configure.

For Intel Pentium CPUs, there are basically two models of processors—the P54C and the P55C.

The P54C is the original Pentium CPU. Most upgraders will choose this version of the Pentium.

The P55C is the newest Pentium, also referred to as the MMX processor. It is just now starting to ship.

If you turn the Pentium CPU on its back with the pins facing you, you'll notice a set of specifications in the center of the chip, as in Figure 5.10.

One of the lines contains the *s-spec* marking. For one of the Pentiums that we have, this line reads as follows:

SX994 / VMU

The last three letters (**VMU**) following the s-spec indicate the voltage setting for this Pentium CPU. The first letter is the important one. If this letter is **S**, then the CPU requires a voltage of from 3.135 to 3.6V. Otherwise, this letter is **V** and the CPU requires a voltage of from 3.4 to 3.6V.

(Figure 5.10)
The s-spec
markings on a
Pentium CPU
are on the bottom

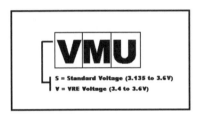

(Figure 5.11) The first letter specifies the CPU voltage

So this Pentium CPU requires a VRE voltage of from 3.4V to 3.6V.

Now we have to take a look at the user manual again and find the jumpers which specify the CPU voltage. Figure 5.12 is a reproduction from the same user's manual.

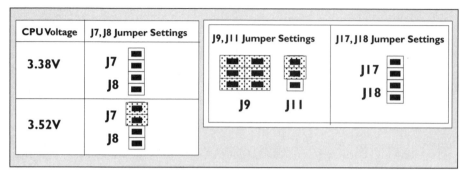

CPU Voltage	J7, J8 Jumper Settings
3.38V	J7 / J8
3.52V	J7 / J8

(Figure 5.12) CPU Voltage settings

Figure 5.12 tells us to set the CPU voltage as follows:

J7	Jumper pins		J11	Jumper top two pins
J8	No jumpers		J17	No jumpers
J9	Jumper three set of pins		J18	No jumpers

For Intel Pentium CPUs which do not have the three-letter suffix following the s-spec, consult the table in Appendix A to determine the voltage.

As Figure 5.13 shows, the voltage setting for a Cyrix 6x86 CPU is stamped right on the front of the CPU—3V or 3.52V.

As you can see, there aren't very many jumpers or switches that we have to set for this motherboard.

Still, you'll have to read the user's manual for details of your particular motherboard. If you have questions about the settings, ask the salesperson or technician from whom you bought the motherboard. They have a lot of experience building PCs and should be familiar with the specific settings for the motherboards they sell.

(Figure 5.13) The Cyrix 6x86 CPU announces the voltage on the front label.

| Step 2 | Install The CPU On The Motherboard |

Installing the CPU is an easy step. All Pentium motherboards have a ZIF socket. ZIF stands for Zero Insertion Force and as its name implies, you don't have to apply any pressure to insert the CPU into its socket.

NOTE

Discharge yourself of any electrostatic energy before you handle the CPU.

At the side of the ZIF socket you'll find a small plastic or metal arm. Unlatch and lift the arm until it is standing upright. You'll notice that there is a small notch on one of the four corners of your Pentium CPU.

Turn the CPU upside down to locate three gold pins that run diagonally to the corner. You'll also see three small holes that run diagonally on one of the corners of the ZIF socket.

These pins and holes indicate the proper alignment of the CPU and socket. You'll only be able to insert the CPU into the socket by aligning the diagonal pins and holes. Carefully insert the CPU into the socket, making sure that the CPU is fully seated. Don't force the CPU into the socket. It will easily drop into place on its own. If it doesn't, wiggle the arm a bit. See Figures 5.14, 5.15 and 5.16.

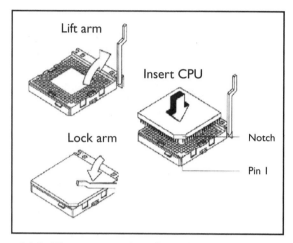

(Figure 5.14) Three steps to installing the CPU in the ZIF socket

(Figure 5.15) Gently place the CPU into the socket

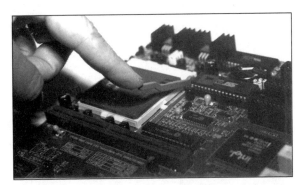

(Figure 5.16) Lower the arm and lock the CPU in place

When the CPU is properly seated in the ZIF socket, lower the arm fully and latch it so that the CPU is locked into place.

Step 3 Install The Cache Memory On The Motherboard

Some motherboards have cache memory preinstalled. Figure 5.17 shows a motherboard that was manufactured with 256K of onboard pipeline burst cache memory.

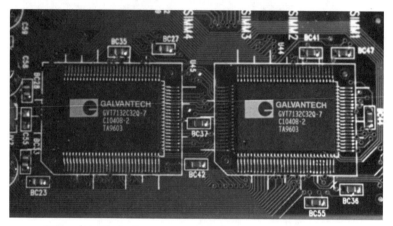

(Figure 5.17) Cache memory is built into this motherboard

Your motherboard may also have onboard cache memory and/or may have one or more sockets for adding cache memory. The cache memory may be individual static RAM chips or COAST modules.

> **NOTE**
>
> Before you handle the cache memory chips or module, make sure that you've discharged yourself of any electrostatic energy.

If your motherboard uses the individual static RAM chips, then install them by aligning the notched corner of the static RAM chip with the notch indicator on the socket and gently pushing the chip into its socket. Be careful not to bend the delicate pins. See Figure 5.18.

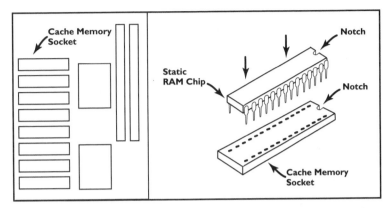

(Figure 5.18) When install static RAM cache, be careful not to bend the pins.

In addition to the onboard cache, this motherboard has a socket which accepts a pipeline burst cache (COAST) module. Installing a COAST module increases the amount of cache memory on this motherboard from 256K to 512K. If you've purchased a COAST module, you can simply plug it into the motherboard. You can only insert the COAST module into its socket in one direction, to prevent you from installing it backwards (see Figure 5.19).

(Figure 5.19) A COAST pipeline burst cache module easily snaps into the socket.

97

Step 4 | Install Memory On The Motherboard

Main memory comes in one of two styles, or *modules*.

1. Conventional 72-pin SIMM

2. Newer 168-pin DIMM

You're probably familiar with 72-pin SIMMs, since they have been widely used in 486 systems for several years.

One of the ways that you'll be able to save money on this upgrade is to reuse the 72-pin SIMMs from your 486. Of course, if your 486 uses the older 30-pin SIMM modules, you'll have to purchase new memory.

SIMM savers

Some dealers stock an item commonly called a *SIMM saver*. A SIMM saver is a small component designed to let you use 30-pin SIMMs on a motherboard which only accepts 72-pin SIMMs. Our experience suggests that SIMM savers only occasionally work as advertised. We aren't strong believers in SIMM savers. Because the price for 72-pin SIMMs is so attractive, SIMM savers no longer represent an attractive way to upgrade your computer. Go for the 72-pin SIMMs, instead.

If your 486 system used 72-pin SIMMs and you haven't done so already, remove the SIMMs from your 486 motherboard. There is a metal clip at each end of the SIMM socket. Gently push the clip out and away from the center of the socket to release its grip on the SIMM. You'll then be able to lift the SIMM out of its socket.

Most motherboards can accept up to four SIMM modules, one in each of the four long light-colored sockets in the upper-right-hand corner of Figure 5.20.

The four sockets are arranged as two *banks* of two sockets each. In our user's manual, a schematic of the sockets indicated that one is labeled Bank 0 and the other Bank 1. If you are installing only two SIMMs, these must be installed in Bank 0. If you want to install additional memory at a later time, you can add two more SIMMs in Bank 1. Make sure that you know which sockets are Bank 0 and which are Bank 1, as in Figure 5.20.

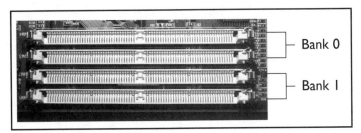

(Figure 5.20) Each bank of memory is made of two SIMM sockets

NOTE

Discharge yourself of electrostatic energy before touching any of the SIMM modules.

Pick up one of the SIMM modules. Find the small holes on each side of the module. Beneath one of the holes you'll see a notch. This notch is designed to prevent you from inserting the SIMM module backwards into a socket. Examine the SIMM socket and note the alignment in which you'll have to insert the SIMM module so that the notch will clear the plastic tab. With the metal fingers pointing down, carefully insert the SIMM module into a socket in Bank 0 so it is properly aligned. The module is inserted into the socket at a 30 degree angle from vertical. The metal fingers will line up perfectly with the fingers in the socket. If you happen to insert the SIMM backwards, the fingers will not align correctly and the notch will not clear the plastic tab. The holes in the SIMM will align with the pegs on the socket and the metal clips of the socket will click to indicate that the SIMM is locked in place. See Figures 5.21 and 5.22.

(Figure 5.21) Here we're inserting a 72-pin SIMM into one of the sockets.

Here's a pictorial view of how the SIMMs are installed:

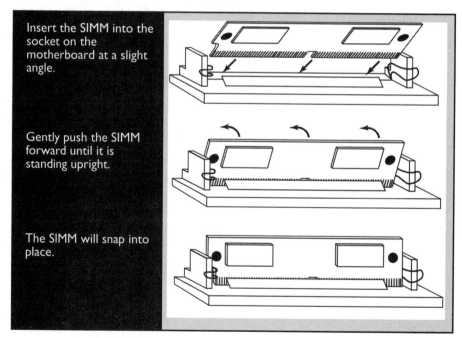

Insert the SIMM into the socket on the motherboard at a slight angle.

Gently push the SIMM forward until it is standing upright.

The SIMM will snap into place.

(Figure 5.22) Installing memory on the motherboard

Remember that SIMM modules must be installed in pairs and that both SIMM modules in the same bank must have the same memory capacity. So for example, to have a 16MB computer system, you would install two 8MB SIMMs into one of the banks or four 4MB SIMMs into both of the banks.

A second type of memory module is a 168-pin DIMM. Figure 5.23 shows the socket on the motherboard which accepts this type of memory.

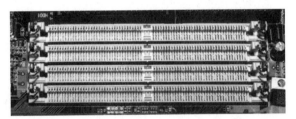

(Figure 5.23) This DIMM socket along the bottom edge accepts a 168-pin memory module. The plastic clips at both ends lock the DIMM in place.

A DIMM module has more "fingers" (168 of them) on its bottom edge. Because of the position of the center notch, you can insert it only one way into the socket.

To install a DIMM memory module, insert the module into the DIMM socket. The socket is "keyed" so that you'll only be able to insert the module in one direction. After you've gently pressed the module into place, fold the plastic clips at the end of the socket over the module to lock it in place.

Step 5   Mount The New Motherboard

Before we continue, let's look at some of the mounting hardware that you'll most likely run across. The most common way of mounting the motherboard in the case is to use plastic *standoffs* and screws. You probably removed a few standoffs when you took the old 486 motherboard out of its case. Here's a picture of several types of standoffs that are commonly used:

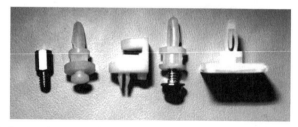

(Figure 5.24) Here's a selection of various standoffs. From left to right: Brass, Standard, Edge, Screw-down, and Adhesive-backed
(Courtesy of Skyline Computers, Brookfield, IL)

The brass and standard standoffs are used for most mounting jobs.

A standoff is not only attaches the motherboard to the case, but also holds the motherboard a safe distance away from the metal chassis to prevent unwanted connections from short circuiting the system.

(Figure 5.25) Brass standoffs and machine mounting screws. The brass standoffs are screwed directly into the case. When secured to the brass standoff with a machine screw, the motherboard is grounded to the case.

You may want to use felt or cork adhesive-backed pads to further protect your motherboard (see Figure 5.26).

When you removed your 486 motherboard in Chapter 4, we asked you to carefully remove the plastic standoffs. We'll be using those standoffs to mount your new motherboard in the case.

The only trick in mounting the motherboard is lining the holes in the chassis up with the holes in the motherboard. An easy way to do this is to take a large piece of paper, scotch tape it to the underside of the chassis and carefully trace the outline of the cutouts and small screw holes with a felt marker.

Note the location of the keyboard connector cutout on the back side of the case's frame on the paper template. Untape the paper from the chassis. It should look similar to Figure 5.27.

(Figure 5.26) A supply of felt pads can come in handy for mounting your motherboard.

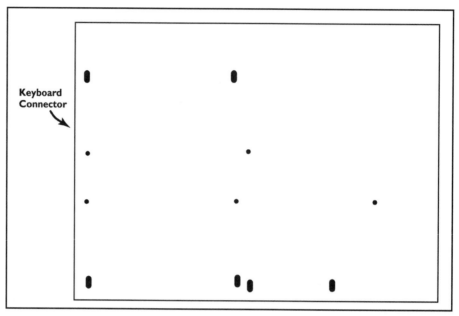

Keyboard
Connector

(Figure 5.27) This paper template indicates the position of the cutouts and screw holes on the chassis.

Now place the motherboard over the paper template so that the keyboard connector is in the same relative position as indicated on the paper template, as in Figure 5.28. Move the motherboard until its holes are aligned with the holes that you traced on the template. Not all of the holes will be lined up. Note those holes that **are** lined up by drawing an "X" on the paper template where the holes line up exactly. These Xs are the points at which you will soon attach the motherboard to the chassis. For a secure installation, you'll want to attach the motherboard to the chassis at a minimum of six or seven points.

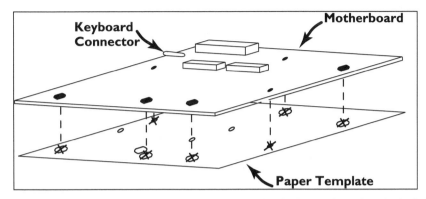

(Figure 5.28) Identify the holes on the motherboard which are aligned with the holes in the case.

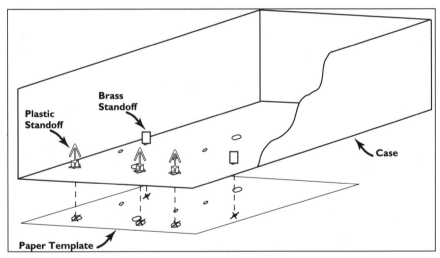

(Figure 5.29) X marks the spot. Plastic and brass standoffs are attached to the case at the Xs.

Now place the paper template beneath the case once again. The Xs on the paper template indicate the points at which the plastic and metal standoffs will attach to the case. See Figure 5.29. Now you'll insert the plastic and metal standoffs in cutouts and holes in the case corresponding to the Xs on the paper template.

To attach a plastic standoff to the chassis, insert the short end of the standoff into the larger end of the oblong cutout and slide it towards the smaller end. Make sure that the sides of the metal opening slide snugly into the plastic groove of the standoff. See Figure 5.30.

(Figure 5.30)   Attaching a standard plastic standoff to the chassis

To attach a metal standoff, simply screw it into the desired chassis aperture. The metal standoffs also ground the motherboard to the case.

Attach the desired number of standoffs to the case. Now gently lower the motherboard into the case and align the holes over the standoffs. First secure the motherboard to the brass standoffs, as in Figure 5.31. Screw the motherboard to each of the brass standoffs with the mounting screws from your accessory package. As you're doing this, you'll see the heads of the plastic standoffs peeking through the holes in the motherboard. When all of the screws have been secured, gently press the motherboard at a point close to each of the plastic standoffs. The top of the plastic standard standoffs will pop through the holes in the motherboard and open up (like an umbrella) to hold the motherboard in place. Tighten the screws again. You've just completed the physical mounting.

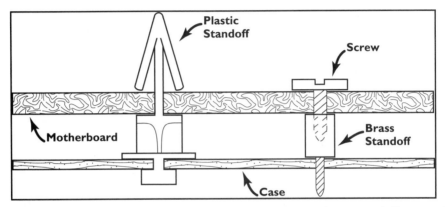

(Figure 5.31)   This side view shows you how the plastic and brass standoffs are used to mount the motherboard to the chassis.

Now check to make sure that no surfaces on the bottom of the motherboard are touching the metal case. If any are, remove the motherboard and reinstall it. Otherwise, the motherboard will short circuit on the case and become damaged. When you're done, the bottom of the case will look similar to this:

(Figure 5.32) A bottom view of the chassis after the motherboard has been mounted to the case using the plastic and brass standoffs.

If you have trouble

Sometimes the holes in the motherboard just will not line up with the cutouts and screw holes on the chassis.

If this happens, you can purchase either screw-down standoffs or adhesive-backed standoffs. Both of these standoffs can be placed anywhere on the chassis. For screw-down standoffs, you'll have to drill a hole in the desired position on the chassis. For the adhesive-backed standoffs, simply remove the protective backing and press the standoff onto the desired position in the case.

Step 6 Reinstall The Power Supply

You may have removed the power supply from your case in Step 7 of Chapter 4. If so, you'll need to reinstall it now.

This procedure is simple enough.

Gently place the power supply into the case. Be absolutely sure that the wire harnesses leading from the power supply are not kinked, bent or caught beneath any of the metal ribs of the case.

Replace and tighten the hex screws that fasten the power supply to the case.

If you also detached the electrical cord from the power supply to the on/off switch, then reconnect it now. Make sure that wires are reattached to the correct connector of the on/off switch.

Step 7 | Connect The Power Supply To The Motherboard

There are six or seven sets of wires (called "harnesses") that lead from the power supply. Locate the two harnesses which have six wires each, whose connectors are labeled "P8" and "P9." These harnesses supply electrical power to the motherboard.

(Figure 5.33) The two wire harnesses in the left foreground labeled "P8" and "P9" have six wires each. These supply electrical power to the motherboard.

The P8 and P9 connectors are designed to attach to the motherboard in only one direction. If the connector does not attach easily, then it's probably backwards. The ribbed side of the P8 and P9 connectors should face the power supply connector on the motherboard. Attach both 6-pin connectors (P8 and P9) to a single 12-pin connector on the motherboard so that the four black wires are located in the middle of the 12-pin connector. Check and double-check to make sure that they're correctly connected so that you won't fry your motherboard.

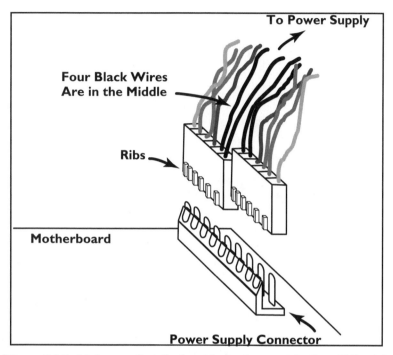

(Figure 5.34) Make sure that the four black wires meet in the middle of the motherboard connector.

Step 8   Connect The Other Case Wires To The Motherboard

In Step 8 of Chapter 4, you detached the remaining case wires from the motherboard.

We noted the colors and purpose of these wires in Table 4-1, which we also reproduce here as Table 5-1.

Wire Sets	Features		Wire Sets	Features
Red/White	HDD Led		Yellow/White	Turbo Led
Green/White	Power Led		Blue/White	Reset switch
Black/Orange	Keylock		Orange/White/Blac	Turbo switch
Red/Black	Speaker			

(Table 5-1)   Wire set connections

In this step we'll have to reverse the procedure. To connect the wires, we'll have to identify the corresponding connectors on the new motherboard. Figure 5.35 is a diagram of the case connectors taken from the user's manual for our motherboard.

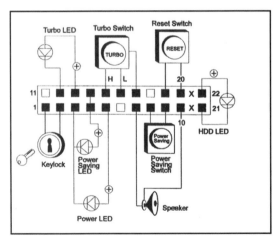

(Figure 5.35)   Case connectors for our motherboard

Now it's just a matter of matching the connector from Table 5.1 with the connector from Figure 5.35.

Wire Sets	Pin numbers		Wire Sets	Pin numbers
Red/White	Pins 21-22		Yellow/White	Pins 12-13
Green/White	Pins 3-5		Blue/White	Pins 19-20
Black/Orange	Pins 1-2		Orange/White/Blac	Pins 15-17
Red/Black	Pins 7-10			

(Table 5-2) Matching the connectors

(Figure 5.36) Case connectors attached to the motherboard

Keep in mind that these connections will likely be different for your case and motherboard. The above connectors are merely used to illustrate how we determined which connections to make.

Step 9 — Install The CPU Cooling Fan

Pentium-class processors generate a lot of heat—much more than a 486-class CPU. You'll have to install a cooling fan to prevent the CPU from overheating and damaging itself.

A CPU cooling fan consists of a metal heat sink and the fan housing. Before installing the cooling fan, make sure that the top of the CPU is clean and free from dirt and grit. If not, gently wipe the top ceramic or metal surface with a clean cloth. To work properly, the heat sink has to make good contact with the top surface of the CPU. Fit the heat sink carefully over the top of the CPU. Next, clip the fan housing over both the heat sink and the CPU, making sure that it is securely fastened to the edge of the ZIF socket. Most fan housings clasp over the edge of the socket.

Plug the cooling fan cable into a power supply connector. Make sure that the other wires or cables do not obstruct the airflow of the fan.

(Figure 5.37) Installing the CPU cooling fan

PAUSE - Tips for installing add-on cards:

Even though you've already added and removed cards from your 486, we'd like to take a short break to describe some techniques for reinstalling add-on cards in the motherboard's expansion slots.

Several of the expansion slot covers on your computer case are already uncovered. If you have to remove additional slot covers, you'll find one of two kinds: perforated slot covers and removable slot covers. Perforated slot covers are stamped into the case's back panel. To remove a slot cover, carefully bend it back and forth until the perforated bottom edge tears away from the panel. As you do this, be careful not to damage any of the tiny components on the motherboard. Figure 5.38 shows how you remove one of the expansion slot covers.

(Figure 5.38) Removing an expansion slot cover from the back panel of the case

In other computer cases, the expansion slot covers are screwed into the back panel. To remove these slot covers, simply unscrew the screw holding the cover in place.

Here's a couple of tips you should follow when installing any card into an expansion slot:

❖ Carefully insert the edge of the card into the slot.

❖ Gently rock the board back and forth from front to back until it seats securely in the slot and the metal fingers are making positive contact.

❖ Ensure that no part of the card is pressing on any of the delicate motherboard components underneath.

❖ Verify that the metal plate on the card aligns perfectly with the back of the case.

❖ Screw the metal plate into the case to complete the physical installation.

Now we're ready to reconnect the peripherals. This motherboard and most motherboards that you'll be using have IDE interfaces onboard. If for some strange reason you have a motherboard without a built-in IDE interface, you'll have to use a separate I/O card. If this is the case, insert it into one of the ISA slots on the motherboard and secure it with a screw to the back of the case. In subsequent steps, when we refer to "connectors on the motherboard," you should substitute "connectors on the I/O board."

If you've removed the drive cage (as in Step 6 of Chapter 4), you can reinstall it now, since the motherboard is securely seated in the case.

Here are the cables that attach peripherals to the motherboard:

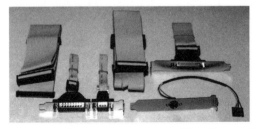

(Figure 5.39)   Here are all of the connecting cables that you'll use to attach peripherals to the motherboard.

Step 10	Reattach The Floppy Drive

A 34-wire ribbon cable is used to connect the floppy drive to the motherboard (or I/O card). In Figure 5.40 you can see that one end of the cable connects to the floppy controller on the motherboard.

The other end has two connectors for the A drive. One of these is for a floppy drive with an edge connector and the other is for a floppy drive that has a 34-pin connector (see Figure 5.41).

In the middle are two connectors for the B drive. Again, one is for an edge connector and the other for a 34-pin connector.

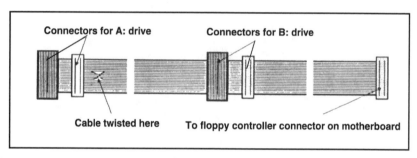

(Figure 5.40) A 34-wire ribbon cable connects a floppy drive to the motherboard or I/O board.

Most likely, your floppy drive will have a 34-pin connector, since the edge connectors are ancient. In any case, plug either the 34-pin connector or the edge connector into the back of the floppy drive. The edge connector on the ribbon is "keyed" so it will fit onto the floppy drive in only one direction. Then plug one of the power supply connectors into the back of the floppy drive.

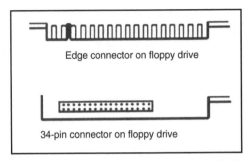

(Figure 5.41) One of two types of connectors is found on the back of a floppy drive.

Along the length of the cable is a color line (usually red) which indicates pin 1 on the connector. Plug the 34-pin connector into the floppy controller port on the motherboard, making sure that pin 1 of the connector matches pin 1 on the board (see Figure 5.43).

(Figure 5.42)   Plug a power supply cable and the 34-pin connector (A-drive) into the floppy drive.

(Figure 5.43) Plug the 34-pin ribbon cable from the floppy drive into the motherboard (or separate I/O board)

Step 11 | Reconnect The IDE Hard Drive

A 40-wire ribbon cable is used to connect the hard drive to the motherboard. This ribbon cable has three 40-pin connectors—one at each end and a third about one-third of the way towards one end, as in Figure 5.44.

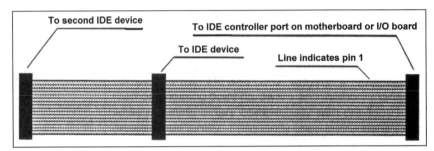

(Figure 5.44) A 40-wire ribbon cable connects IDE devices to the motherboard or I/O board.

A color line (usually red) along the length of the cable ribbon indicates pin 1, similar to the 34-pin floppy cable. Plug one end of the 40-pin connector into the motherboard's primary IDE controller connector, making sure that pin 1 of the connector matches pin 1 on the board.

(Figure 5.45) Plug the 40-pin connector into the motherboard (or separate I/O board)

Plug the other end of the cable into the connector on the hard drive, again making sure that pin 1 on the cable matches pin 1 of the hard drive. Plug one of the power supply connectors into the hard drive (see Figure 5.46).

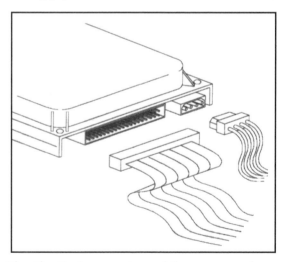

(Figure 5.46) Plug the 40-pin connector and the power supply connector into the back of the hard drive.

The Upgrade

Step 12 | Reinstall The Sound Card/CD-ROM Controller And Drive

There are two kinds of expansion slots on your motherboard: ISA and PCI.

The ISA slots are the longer of the two, about 5-1/2" in length. These are the same slots that are in your 486 motherboard. Most ISA slots are dark colored.

The PCI slots are shorter, measuring about 3" in length. In general, PCI slots are light colored.

Our 486 system had a combination sound card/CD-ROM controller. This was a very popular way to add multimedia capabilities to computers two years ago.

We don't have to change any jumpers on this card since we're not adding new cards (excepting the video display card). Reinstall the sound card/CD-ROM controller by inserting it into a vacant ISA slot.

Next we plug one end of the CD-ROM cable into the controller and the other end of the cable into the CD-ROM drive. Make sure that a power supply cable is also attached to the CD-ROM drive.

A second four-wire cable connects the CD-ROM drive to a small connector on the sound card. This cable enables you to play music CDs directly through the sound card.

Step 13	Reinstall The Ethernet Network Card

Our 486 was originally connected to a network.

Insert the network interface card into an ISA slot and attach the card to the back of the case with a screw. We don't have to change any jumpers on the card since we won't be adding new cards (again, excepting the video display card).

Step 14 · Install The Video Display Card

This motherboard has four PCI slots (white) and three ISA/EISA slots (brown). Since we are going to use a PCI video display card, insert the card into one of the PCI slots. Secure the card to the back of the case with a screw.

(Figure 5.47) Insert the video display card into a PCI slot.

Like most others, we did not have to change any settings on this video display card.

<table>
<tr><td>**Step
15**</td><td>Connect The Serial Ports To The Motherboard</td></tr>
</table>

Our new motherboard has I/O capabilities built in. If you're using a separate I/O board, then you'll have these same I/O features.

These include two serial communication ports, which mount on the back panel of the case. There are usually removable knockouts on the back panel for various connectors, either 9-pin or 25-pin. Both are male gender. Remove one or both of the knockouts for the desired connector size.

(Figure 5.48) Securing a 9-pin serial port connector to the back of the case

Mount the metal connector(s) to the case with two hex screws, as in Figure 5.48. A flat ribbon runs from this connector and attaches to the motherboard with a 10-pin plastic connector. The motherboard connectors are usually clearly labeled. Plug the connector into either the COM1 or COM2 connectors. Be sure that pin 1 on the motherboard corresponds to pin 1 on the cable (the colored line indicates pin 1).

The serial ports are now ready for use.

Step 16 | Connect The Parallel Port To The Motherboard

In addition to the two serial ports, the I/O capabilities of this motherboard include a parallel port—sometimes called a printer port.

The parallel port is a 25-pin female connector that usually mounts onto the back panel of the case. Remove one of the knockouts for this size connector.

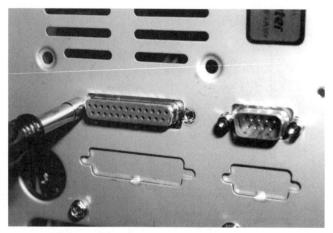

(Figure 5.49) Secure the parallel port connector to the back of the case.

Mount the connector to the back panel of the case, as in Figure 5.49. A flat ribbon runs from this connector to the motherboard and attaches with a 26-pin plastic connector. The motherboard connectors are usually clearly labeled with the word "PARALLEL" or "PRINTER." Be sure that pin 1 on the motherboard corresponds to pin 1 on the cable (the colored line indicates pin 1).

The parallel port is now ready for use.

Step 17	Connect The Mouse

There are two classes of mice: serial and PS/2 style.

Serial mouse

A serial mouse plugs into one of the two serial ports. In step 15, we connected the serial ports to the motherboard. If your mouse is a serial variety, plug it into the 9-pin connector.

If your mouse was originally connected to COM1, make sure that the 9-pin port is plugged into the COM1 connector on the motherboard. If it's not, reverse the cables from the 9-pin and 25-pin connectors

Otherwise, if your mouse was originally connected to COM2, make sure that the 9-pin port is plugged into the COM2 connector on the motherboard. If it's not, simply reverse the cables from the 9-pin and 25-pin connectors.

PS/2 style mouse

Many motherboards also have a connector for a PS/2-style mouse port. If you have a PS/2-style mouse, you should set your system to use this type of mouse.

The connector for the PS/2-style mouse is mounted onto a metal expansion slot cover. A narrow ribbon cable (or wire harness) runs between this connector and the motherboard.

Plug the six-pin connector into the appropriate connector on the motherboard (J10 on our motherboard), making sure that pin 1 on the motherboard corresponds to pin 1 on the connector (the colored line indicates pin 1). Next, mount the expansion slot cover with the mouse port onto the back panel of the case, as in Figure 5.50.

Finally, plug the mouse into the mouse port, as in Figure 5.51.

127

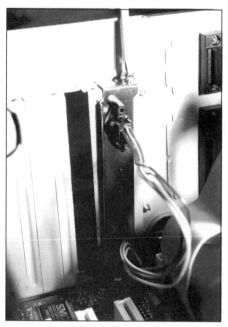

(Figure 5.50) Securing the mouse port to the case

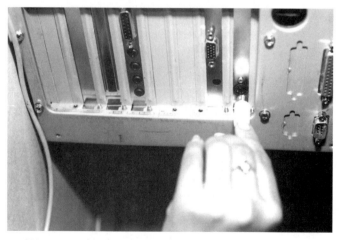

(Figure 5.51) Plug the mouse into the PS/2 mouse port.

128

Step 18	Connect The Monitor To The Video Display Card

We installed the video display card into our computer system in Step 14.

The 15-pin connector for the monitor is now at the back panel of the case. Plug the monitor cable into the video display card connector.

Also plug the monitor power cord into a grounded electrical outlet.

(Figure 5.52) Connecting the monitor

The keyboard connector is attached directly to the motherboard. When you mount the motherboard in the case, the connector is aligned with a cutout in the case.

(Figure 5.53) Plug the keyboard cable into the keyboard connector on the back of the case.

Plug the keyboard into this connector, as in Figure 5.53.

Step 20 Check And Double-check The Connections; Then Clean Up

We're almost ready to turn on the computer. But first, we're asking you to carefully inspect and review your work.

Go back and review steps six through nineteen.

This may seem like an unnecessary thing to do, but by rereading and inspecting your work, you will help insure that you've done things correctly.

Things that you want to especially look for:

Make sure that the bottom side of the motherboard is not touching any metal parts.

Look for loose wires that may be touching the motherboard. A short circuit can damage the system.

Move unused power supply connectors away from other components. You can rubber band these to hold them out of the way.

Step 21 Turn On The Power

You're now ready to try out the new computer. We're going to separate this step into two parts. The first part is for users upgrading a 486 system that originally ran DOS 6.22 and Windows 3.11. The second part is for an upgrade to a 486 system that originally used Windows 95.

Part one: When you're upgraded a DOS 6.22/ Windows 3.11 system

The hard drive contains our original DOS 6.22 operating system and also runs Windows 3.11, so we're expecting that our newly upgraded computer will be able to boot directly to DOS.

1. Remove any diskettes from the floppy drive(s).

2. Turn on the power to the monitor.

3. Next turn on the power to the computer.

When we first turn our computer on, we see the following message:

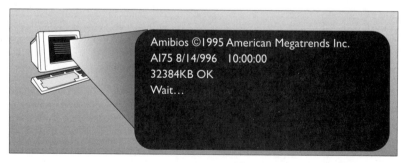

```
Amibios ©1995 American Megatrends Inc.
AI75 8/14/996   10:00:00
32384KB OK
Wait...
```

This message is a good sign. It means that the motherboard is functioning correctly and the video display card and monitor are working.

The message is from the BIOS built into the motherboard and is telling us that it has found 32MB of memory (the amount of memory that you install may differ).

Next the BIOS displays this message:

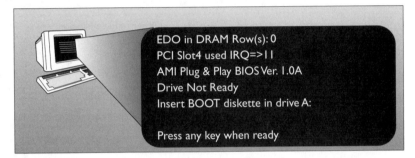

```
EDO in DRAM Row(s): 0
PCI Slot4 used IRQ=>11
AMI Plug & Play BIOS Ver. 1.0A
Drive Not Ready
Insert BOOT diskette in drive A:

Press any key when ready
```

Now the BIOS has recognized floppy drive A. This is another good sign, telling us the floppy drive installed properly. Since we have a DOS diskette, we insert it into the drive to load DOS and press a key.

At this point, the BIOS hasn't recognized our hard drive(s). Why not?

The answer is because we haven't setup the BIOS parameters. When the system is first turned on, you will see a message similar to this:

```
Hit DEL if you want to run SETUP
```

The BIOS only gives you a few seconds to press the Del key so you have to be fast. Restart your system by turning it off and then on again. Press the Del key when prompted to enter the BIOS SETUP program.

When the SETUP program starts, you'll see a menu of several options:

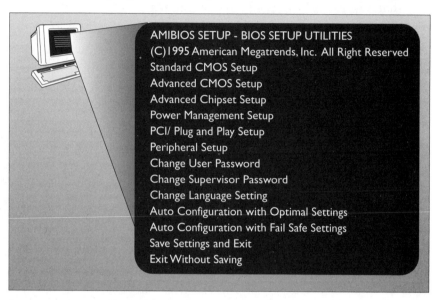

AMIBIOS SETUP - BIOS SETUP UTILITIES
(C)1995 American Megatrends, Inc. All Right Reserved
Standard CMOS Setup
Advanced CMOS Setup
Advanced Chipset Setup
Power Management Setup
PCI/ Plug and Play Setup
Peripheral Setup
Change User Password
Change Supervisor Password
Change Language Setting
Auto Configuration with Optimal Settings
Auto Configuration with Fail Safe Settings
Save Settings and Exit
Exit Without Saving

Choose **Standard CMOS Setup**. You'll see a screen similar to this one:

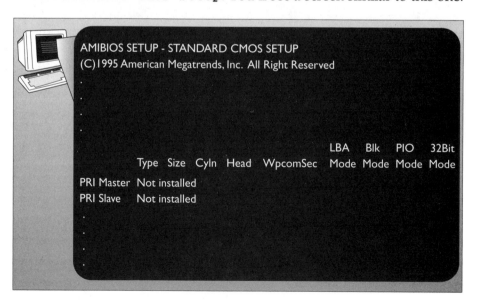

AMIBIOS SETUP - STANDARD CMOS SETUP
(C)1995 American Megatrends, Inc. All Right Reserved

	Type	Size	Cyln	Head	WpcomSec	LBA Mode	Blk Mode	PIO Mode	32Bit Mode
PRI Master	Not installed								
PRI Slave	Not installed								

Regardless of which BIOS utility is built into your motherboard, you'll be able to change the type of fixed disks. You'll probably use the arrow keys or [Tab] to move the cursor to the field labeled **TYPE** of PRI Master. Then you'll want to change the value from "Not Installed" to "**AUTO**." If you have a second hard drive, you should change it's **TYPE** to "**AUTO**" also. This **AUTO** setting instructs the BIOS to automatically select the drive type and parameters each time the system is turned on. After we made these changes, the screen displayed the following:

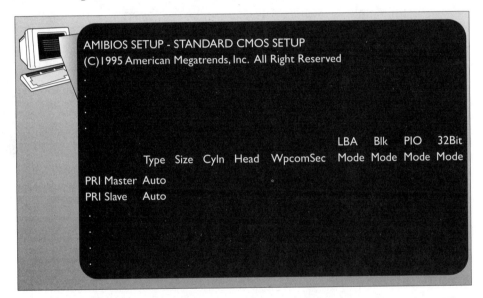

AMIBIOS SETUP - STANDARD CMOS SETUP
(C)1995 American Megatrends, Inc. All Right Reserved

	Type	Size	Cyln	Head	WpcomSec	LBA Mode	Blk Mode	PIO Mode	32Bit Mode
PRI Master	Auto								
PRI Slave	Auto								

Now that we've reset the hard drive types, we exit from this screen. This is usually done by pressing the [Esc] key. Then we choose the option to **Save Settings and Exit**. The system restarts and this time recognizes the hard drive(s). We immediately know that the drives are recognized because the BIOS displays the type and manufacturer of the drive(s) such as:

135

This is a message from the BIOS telling us that is has recognized our two hard drives (a Maxtor and an IBM).

After displaying these two messages, the system continued with these messages:

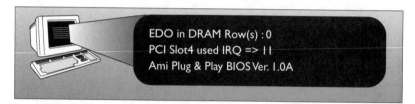

Unfortunately, our computer would not go any further. As it turns out, we ran into a problem with our Maxtor 7540 AV hard drive. When it was part of our 486 system, it was configured as a standard drive that did not use *LBA mode*. After we upgraded the system to a Pentium and chose "**AUTO**" for the type of PRI Master drive, our BIOS automatically set this drive to LBA mode.

To fix this problem, we went back into the BIOS setup utility and changed the field **TYPE** of PRI Master from "**AUTO**" to "**USER**." Then we moved to the field labeled "**LBA MODE**" and changed the value from **ON** to **OFF**. After saving these parameters and exiting, the system boots normally and we are back in business—only this time with a super-fast Pentium processor running Windows 3.11 instead of our old slow-poke 486.

We can't say whether you'll run into this same problem, but now you'll know how to solve it if you do.

Part two:
When you've upgraded a Windows 95 system

We also upgraded a second 486 system which was originally running Windows 95. We followed the exact same procedures to upgrade from a 486 to a Pentium and now we're ready to turn on the power.

1. Remove any diskettes from the floppy drive(s).

2. Turn on the power to the monitor.

3. Next turn on the power to the computer.

When we first turn our computer on, we see the following message:

This message is a good sign. It means that the motherboard is functioning correctly and the video display card and monitor are working.

The message is from the BIOS built into the motherboard and is telling us that it has found 32MB of memory (the amount of memory that you install may differ).

Next the BIOS displays this message:

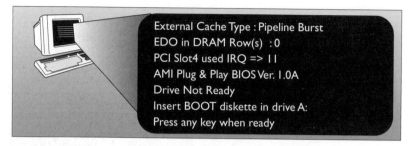

External Cache Type : Pipeline Burst
EDO in DRAM Row(s) : 0
PCI Slot4 used IRQ => 11
AMI Plug & Play BIOS Ver. 1.0A
Drive Not Ready
Insert BOOT diskette in drive A:
Press any key when ready

Now the BIOS has recognized floppy drive A. This is another good sign; the floppy drive installed properly. Since we have a DOS boot diskette, we insert it into the floppy drive to load DOS and press a key.

At this point, the BIOS hasn't recognized our hard drive(s). Why not?

The answer is because we haven't setup the BIOS parameters. When the system is first turned on, you will see a message similar to this:

Hit DEL if you want to run SETUP

The BIOS only gives you a few seconds to press the [Del] key so you have to be fast. Restart your system by turning it off and then on again. Press the [Del] key when prompted to enter the BIOS SETUP program.

When the SETUP program starts, you are presented with a menu of several options:

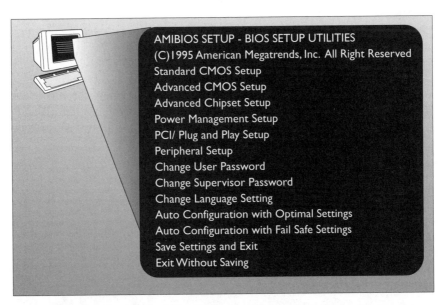

AMIBIOS SETUP - BIOS SETUP UTILITIES

(C)1995 American Megatrends, Inc. All Right Reserved

Standard CMOS Setup
Advanced CMOS Setup
Advanced Chipset Setup
Power Management Setup
PCI/ Plug and Play Setup
Peripheral Setup
Change User Password
Change Supervisor Password
Change Language Setting
Auto Configuration with Optimal Settings
Auto Configuration with Fail Safe Settings
Save Settings and Exit
Exit Without Saving

Choose **Standard CMOS Setup**. You'll see a screen similar to this one:

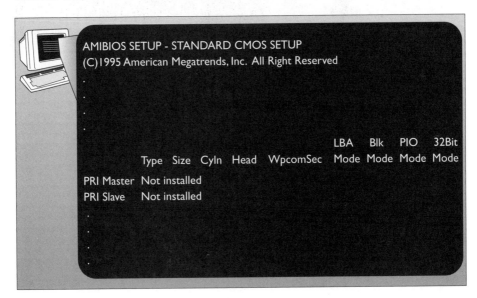

AMIBIOS SETUP - STANDARD CMOS SETUP

(C)1995 American Megatrends, Inc. All Right Reserved

	Type	Size	Cyln	Head	Wpcom	Sec	LBA Mode	Blk Mode	PIO Mode	32Bit Mode
PRI Master	Not installed									
PRI Slave	Not installed									

Regardless of which BIOS utility is built into your motherboard, you'll be able to change the type of fixed disks. You'll probably use the arrow keys or ⟨Tab⟩ to move the cursor to the field **TYPE** of PRI Master. Then you'll want to change the value from "Not Installed" to "**AUTO**." For this computer system BIOS, the ⟨Pg Up⟩ and ⟨Pg Dn⟩ keys are used to change the values in a field. If you have a second hard drive, change it's **TYPE** to "**AUTO**" also. This **AUTO** setting instructs the BIOS to automatically select the type of drive and parameters each time the system is turned on. After we make these changes, the system reboots and the screen displays the following:

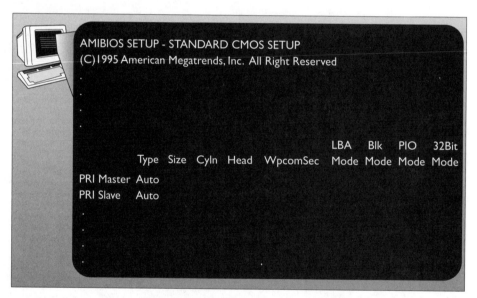

Now that we've reset the hard drive types, we exit from this screen. This is usually done by pressing the ⟨Esc⟩ key. Then we choose the option to **Save Settings and Exit**. The system restarts and this time recognizes the hard drive(s). We immediately know that the drives are recognized because the BIOS displays the type and manufacturer of the drive, such as:

This is a message from the BIOS telling us that is has recognized our two hard drives (a Maxtor and an IBM).

After displaying these two messages, the system continued with these messages:

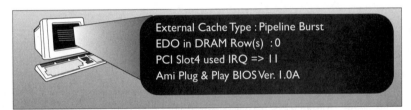

Unfortunately, our computer would not go any further. This message appears on the screen:

It turns out that we have a problem with our Maxtor 7540 AV hard drive from which we are trying to load the Windows 95 operating system. When it was part of our 486 system, it was configured as a standard drive that did not use *LBA mode*. After we upgraded the system to a Pentium and chose "**AUTO**" for the type of PRI Master drive, our BIOS automatically sets this drive to LBA mode.

To fix this problem, we went back into the BIOS setup utility and changed the field **TYPE** of PRI Master from "**AUTO**" to "**USER**." Then we to the field labeled "**LBA MODE**" and changed the value from **ON** to **OFF**. After saving these parameters and exiting, the system boots from the hard drive and we are back in business—almost.

Actually, as Windows 95 continues to load, we run into another small problem. When Windows 95 is installed on a computer, it keeps track of all of the hardware devices in its registry. As a 486, we had a Cirrus Logic video display adapter. When we upgraded the computer, we installed a new PCI video display adapter. And now Windows 95 knows that we have a new hardware device that doesn't match the registry.

This isn't much of a problem. To eliminate the message, we double-click My Computer/Control Panel /Add New Hardware.

Use the Add New Hardware Wizard to select the video display adapter card that you've installed in the new Pentium system. For our new system, we choose a Trident video display adapter.

After you've installed the new video display adapter, you can remove the obsolete video display adapter from the Windows 95 registry. Start by double-clicking My Computer/Control Panel/System.

Click on the Device Manager tab and then Display adapters. Highlight the obsolete entry and then click (Remove).

That's all there is to our upgrade. We're now running Windows—only this time with a super fast Pentium processor running Windows 95 instead of the ancient 486.

If you have trouble: Things to check

Screen is blank when the system is turned on

✳ Power supply is not plugged into an electrical outlet

✳ Monitor is not plugged into electrical outlet

✳ Monitor is not turned on

✳ Monitor is not plugged into the video display card

✳ Video display card is not properly seated

✳ SIMMs are not properly seated in their sockets

✳ SIMMs are not installed in pairs

✳ Motherboard is not connected to power supply

✳ Floppy cable is not properly connected to the floppy drive

✳ Floppy cable is not properly connected to the motherboard (or I/O board)

✳ Hard drive cable is not properly connected to the hard drive

✳ Hard drive cable is not properly connected to the motherboard (or I/O board)

Screen displays BIOS startup message but then "hangs" before DOS is loaded

✻ Hard drive is not plugged into IDE port

✻ Power cable is not plugged into the hard drive

✻ Power cable is not plugged into the floppy drive

✻ Floppy drive is not plugged into the floppy controller cable

✻ Floppy controller cable is plugged in backwards

✻ Floppy controller cable is B drive instead of A drive

✻ Hard drive controller cable is plugged in backwards

✻ Boot sequence for the hard drive must be A,C, so it will load DOS from the floppy drive. This is set using BIOS setup. For our computer, we press Del during system startup to enter BIOS setup.

✻ BIOS fixed drive parameters are not set correctly. Try AUTO for type drive.

✻ Make sure that post-update LBA mode matches pre-update LBA mode (ON or OFF).

Getting More Information

Chapter 6

Chapter 6

Getting More Information

BOOKS

Upgrading & Maintaining Your PC, 6th Edition written by Schueller and Veddler; published by Abacus, 1997, ISBN 1-55755-329-7, $44.95 with CD-ROM

Win95 Rx written by Kober, Buechel and Baecker; published by Abacus, 1996, ISBN 1-55755-297-5, $34.95 w/CD-ROM

Upgrading and Repairing PCs, 5th Edition written by Scott Mueller; published by Que, 1995, ISBN 0-7897-0321-1, $49.95 with CD-ROM

The Winn L. Rosch Hardware Bible, 3rd Edition written by Winn Rosch; published by SAMs Publishing, 1994, ISBN 1-56686-127-6, $35.00.

Upgrade & Maintain your PC written by James Karney; published by MID Press, ISBN 1-55828-294-7, 1994, $34.95 with diskette

The Complete PC Upgrade & Maintenance Guide written by Mark Minasi; published by Sybex, 1993, $24.95.

6

OTHER REFERENCES

Byte Magazine

One Phoenix Mill Lane
Peterborough, NH 03458
Phone (603) 924-9281
Toll free (800) 257-9402
Fax (603) 924-2550
http://www.byte.com

Compu-Mart Magazine

899 Presidential
Suite 110
Richardson, TX 75081
Phone (214) 238-1133
Toll free (800) 864-1155
Fax (214) 238-1132

Computer Direct

P.O. Box 55886
Birmingham, AL 35255
Phone (205) 988-9708
Toll free (800) 366-0676
Fax (205) 987-3237

Computer Shopper

One Park Avenue
New York, NY 10016
Phone (212) 503-3900
Toll free (800) 274-6384
Fax (212) 503-3995

Nuts & Volts Magazine

430 Princeland Court
Corona, CA 91719
Phone (909) 371-8497
Toll free (800) 783-4624
Fax (909) 371-3052
http://www.nutsvolts.com

PC Novice Magazine

P.O. Box 85380
Lincoln, NE 68501
Toll Free (800) 472-3500

Processor

P.O. Box 85518
Lincoln, NE 68501
Phone (402) 479-2141
Toll Free (800) 334-7443
Fax (402) 477-9252

SOFTWARE TOOLS AND DIAGNOSTICS

First Aid 95 Deluxe

Software that detects and fixes hundreds of Windows 95 problems.

> CyberMedia Inc.
> 3000 Ocean Park Blvd
> Suite 2001
> Santa Monica, CA 90405
> Phone (310) 581-4700
> Fax (310) 581-4720
> http://www.cybermedia.com

Micro-Scope 6.1

Software that helps you diagnose problems with a PC.

This software works regardless of the operating system which may be installed and checks CPU, memory, IRQs, DMAs, BIOS, hard drives, floppy drives, video cards, more.

> Micro 2000
> 1100 E Broadway
> Suite 301
> Glendale, CA 91205
> Toll-free (800) 864-8008
> Phone (818) 547-0125
> Fax (818) 547-0397
> http://www.micro2000.com

PC Snoop

A hard disk and floppy disk diagnostic and repair utility

Computer Intelligence Corp
42015 Ford Rd
Suite 262
Canton, MI 48187-3529
Phone (313) 981-9630
Fax (313) 981-9634
http://www.adcomm.com/pcsnoop/

Post-Probe

A plug-in card that helps to troubleshoot problems in "dead" PCs. The LEDs on the card identify problem areas.

Micro 2000
1100 E Broadway
Suite 301
Glendale, CA 91205
Toll-free (800) 864-8008
Phone (818) 547-0125
Fax (818) 547-0397
http://www.micro2000.com

MANUFACTURERS AND SUPPLIERS

Where can I buy components?

There are loads of places which sell computer components.

Computer Stores

Most local computer stores build custom computers to order. These local computer stores also sell components. Many times these components are of the *OEM* variety, that is they are not packaged in fancy boxes, but are bulk packed to reduce costs. The quality of these components is usually as high as the equivalent retail packaged components.

Computer Superstores

Computer "superstores" such as Best Buy, Circuit City, CompUSA, ElekTek, Frys, Micro Center and others also sell components. These stores usually sell retail packaged components and are noted for competitive prices and quality products and have standard return policies for defective merchandise.

Computer Shows

Another attractive place to buy components is at one of the many computer shows. These are sometimes called expos, fairs, flea markets or swap meets and are held in many cities nationwide — usually on weekends. At these shows, dozens of small hardware and software vendors sell everything from ink refill kits and paper for your printer, to motherboards, memory, add-on cards and complete computer systems, often at deeply discounted prices.

Since most of these vendors participate in the shows regularly and welcome repeat business, they stand behind the quality and performance of the components which they sell. As is the case with all purchases, don't buy a component based solely on its price. Rather, buy a component because it meets your exact requirements and because you feel that a given vendor can meet those needs satisfactorily.

Check your local newspapers and computer bulletin boards for the location of these shows.

Mail Order / Phone Order

You can also buy components from mail order firms. An especially large source of mail order companies is found in "rags" such as Computer Shopper and Nuts & Volts. Other monthly magazines have extensive ads from components suppliers. Check these publications to find a list of mail order (and toll-free 800 number) hardware component dealers. You can usually buy those "hard to find" components from many of the mail order electronic parts suppliers.

On the next pages is a list of manufacturers and suppliers of components and accessories which you may contact to find out more about their products.

Abrams Computer Industries

444 Lake Cook Road
Suite 1
Deerfield, IL 60015
Phone (847) 267-0644
Fax (847) 940-7715

Supplier of motherboards, CPUs (including Cyrix 6x86), memory

Acer Labs

4701 Patrick Henry Drive
Santa Clara, Ca 95054
Phone (408) 764-0644
Fax (408) 496-6142
http://www.acer.com

Motherboards and chipsets

Advanced Integration Research

2188 Del Franco Street
San Jose, CA 95131
Phone (408) 428-0800
Fax (408) 428-0950
http://www.airwebs.com

Manufacturer of motherboards

Alltech Electronics

2618 Temple Heights
Oceanside, CA 92056
Phone (619) 724-2404
Fax (619) 724-8808
http://www.allelec.com

Supplier of electronics components and parts

Alltronics

2300 Zanker Road
San Jose, CA 95131
Phone (408) 943-9773
Fax (408) 943-9776
http://www.alltronics.com

Supplier of electronics components and parts

Alternative Computer Solutions

Naperville, IL 60565
Phone (708) 420-9921
Fax (708) 420-9312

Supplier of memory

AMD Corporation

One AMD Place
Sunnyvale, CA 94088
Phone (408) 749-5703
Fax (408) 774-7024
http://www.amd.com

Manufacturer of CPUs

American Megatrends International

6145-F Northbelt Pkwy
Norcross, GA 30071
Phone (770) 246-8600
Toll free 800-U-BUY-AMI
Fax (770) 246-8790
http://www.megatrends.com

BIOS

Amtech Computers

4005 Carpenter Road
Ypsilanti, MI 48197
Phone (313) 677-6868
Fax (313) 677-8778

Supplier of motherboards, CPUs, memory, add-on cards, cases, peripherals

A.R.E. Electronics

15272 State Route 12 East
Findlay, OH 45840
Phone (419) 422-1588
Fax (419) 422-4432

Supplier of cables, connectors, tools, switch boxes, hardware.

Astra Computer Corp.

4803 Donald Avenue
Richmond Hts, OH 44143
Phone (216) 691-9551
Fax (216) 691-9756

Supplier of motherboards, CPUs, memory, add-on cards, peripherals, cases

ASUS Computers International

721 Charcot Avenue
San Jose, CA 95131
Phone (408) 474-0567
Fax (408) 474-0568
http://www.asus.com

Manufacturer of motherboards

154

Avery Distributors

3685 Stone School Rd
Ann Arbor, MI 48108
Phone (313) 677-5844
gersha@aol.com

Supplier of memory

Award Software International

777 East Middlefield Rd
Mountain View, CA 94043
Phone (415) 968-4433
Fax (415) 968-0774
http://www.award.com
BIOS

Compuparts Laboratory, Inc.

201 E Cripe Street
South Bend, IN 46637
Phone (219) 243-0421
Fax (219) 243-0422

Supplier motherboards, CPUs, memory, add-on cards

Cyrix Corporation

P.O. Box 850118
Richardson, TX 75085
Phone (214) 968-8388
Toll free (800) 462-9749
Fax (214) 699-9857
http://www.cyrix.com

Manufacturer of CPUs

Digi-Key Corp.

701 Brooks Ave South
Thief River, MN 56701
Toll-free (800) 334-4530
Fax (218) 681-3380

Supplier of connectors, cables, tools, electronic components and switches.

Digilink Technology

3050 Lake Lansing Rd
Suite B
East Lansing, MI 48823
Tel (517) 333-9888
Fax (517) 333-9988

Supplier of motherboards, memory, add-on cards, peripherals, cases

155

Discount Computer, Inc.

10021 Telegraph Road
Redford, MI 48239
Phone (313) 531-3241
Fax (313) 531-1717

Supplier of motherboards, memory, add-on cards, peripherals, cases

DTK Ltd

1035 Centennial Avenue
Picataway, NJ 08854
Phone (908) 562-8800
Fax (908) 562-8400
http://www.dtk.com

Manufacturer of BIOs and motherboards

D.W. Technologies

P.O. Box 4061
Dearborn, MI 48126
Phone (313) 361-6939
Fax (313) 361-6939

Supplier of motherboards, CPUs, memory, add-on cards, peripherals.

Expert Computer

14510 11 Mile Road
Warren, MI 48089
Phone (810) 445-6133
Fax (810) 455-6132

Supplier of motherboards, CPUs, memory, add-on cards, peripherals, cases

GPC Computers

2240 28th Street SE
Grand Rapids, MI 49508
Phone (616) 452-8948
Fax (616) 452-8819

Supplier of motherboards, CPUs, memory, add-on cards, peripherals, cases

Halted Electronics Supply

3500 Ryder Street
Santa Clara, CA 95051
Phone (408) 732-1573
Toll free (800) 442-3833
Fax (408) 732-6428
http://www.halted.com

Supplier of electronics components and parts

Hi-Tech Business Machines

5324 West 79th Street
Indianapolis, IN 46268
Phone (317) 872-6658
Toll free (800) 335-8302
http://www.hi-tech.net

Memory, add-on cards, peripherals, cases.

Intel Corporation

2200 Mission College Blvd
Santa Clara, CA 95052
Phone (408) 528-4725
Fax (408) 765-9904

Manufacturer of CPUs and chipsets

IQ's Technology

15417 West Warren
Dearborn, MI 48126
Phone (313) 581-0506
Fax (313) 581-8841

Supplier of motherboards, memory, add-on cards, peripherals, cases.

JDR Microdevices

1850 South 10th Street
San Jose, CA 95112-4108
Phone (408) 494-1400
Toll free (800) 538-5000
Fax (408) 494-1420

Supplier of hardware, cases, power supplies, keyboards, cables, tools, networking

JK Lee Corporation

1198 E. Dundee Road
Palatine, IL 60067
Phone (847) 358-7115
Fax (847) 358-7115

Supplier of memory and CPUs

M Technologies Inc

1931 Hartog Drive
San Jose, CA 95131
Phone (408) 441-8818
http://www.mtiusa.com

Manufacturer of motherboards

MCM Electronics

650 Congress Park Dr
Centerville, OH 45459-4072
Phone (513) 434-0031
Toll free (800) 543-4330
Fax (513) 434-6959

Supplier of hardware, cases, power supplies, keyboards, cables, tools, networking, electronics parts

Marvic International Inc.

768 East 93rd Street
Brooklyn, NY 11236
Phone (718) 346-7822
Toll Free (800) 678-8128
Fax (718) 346-0438

Supplier of hardware, cases, power supplies, keyboards, cables, tools, networking

Mikon Computers

13604 Merriman Rd.
Livonia, MI 48150
Phone (313) 266-5544
Fax (313) 266-7788

Supplier of motherboards, CPUs, memory, add-on cards, peripherals, cases

Microid Research

2336-D Walsh Ave
Santa Clara, CA 95051
http://www.mrbios.com

Manufacturers of BIOS

Microland Computers

9509 N. Milwaukee Ave
Niles, IL 60714
Phone (847) 966-2300
Fax (847) 966-2368

Supplier of motherboards, CPUs, add-on cards

Norton Computer Sytems, Inc.

4129 W Saginaw
Lansing, MI 48917
Phone (517) 323-3170
Fax (517) 323-2495

Supplier of cables, connectors, tools, switch boxes, hardware.

Opti, Inc.

2525 Walsh Avenue
Santa Clara, Ca 95051
Phone (408) 980-8174
Fax (408) 980-8860
http://www.opti.com

Chipsets

Phoenix Technologies Ltd

2770 De La Cruz
Santa Clara, CA 95050
Phone (408) 654-9000
Fax (408) 452-1985
http://www.ptldt.com

BIOS

Prime Electronic Components

150 West Industry Court
Deer Park, NY 11729
Phone (516) 254-0101
Fax (516) 242-8995
http://www.imsworld.com/prime/

Supplier of electronics components and parts

RA Enterprises

2260 De La Cruz Blvd
Santa Clara, CA 95050
Phone (408) 986-8286
Toll free (800) 801-0230
Fax (408) 986-1009

Supplier of electronics components and parts

Sam's Computers

5218 Wilson Mills Road
Cleveland, OH 44143
Phone (216) 449-1107
Fax (216) 449-3795

Supplier of motherboards, CPUs, memory, add-on cards

Silicon Integrated Systems (SIS)

204 North Wolfe Road
Sunnyvale, CA 94086
Phone (408) 730-5600
Fax (408) 730-5639

Manufacturer of chipsets

Skyline Computerware

3749 Grand Blvd
Brookfield, IL 60513
Phone (708) 387-1064
Fax (708) 387-1063

Supplier of standoffs and other small hardware, cooling fans, cables, add-on cards

Sky-Tech Computers

28480 Southfield Road
Lathrup Village, MI 48076
Phone (810) 559-6932
Fax (810) 559-0827

Supplier of motherboards, CPUs, memory, add-on cards, peripherals, cases

Stone Computer, Inc.

3301 W. Central Avenue
Suite 1-C
Toledo, OH 43606
Phone (419) 536-5299
Fax (419) 536-5406

Supplier of motherboards, CPUs, memory, add-on cards, peripherals, cases

Super Micro

2178 Paragon Drive
San Jose, Ca 95131
Phone (408) 451-1118
Fax (408) 451-1110
http://www.supermicro.com

Manufacturer of motherboards

The Computer Connection

401 N. Main Street
Polk, OH 44866
Phone (419) 945-2877
Fax (419) 945-1342

Supplier of motherboards, CPUs, memory, add-on cards, peripherals, cases

Tynan Computers

1753 S. Main Street
San Jose, CA 95035
Phone (408) 956-8000
Fax (408) 956-8044
http://www.tynan.com

Manufacturer of motherboards

Wintergreen Systems, Inc.

3315 W. 96th Street
Indianapolis, IN 46268
Phone (317) 872-1974
Fax (317) 872-4686
//http:www.in.net/wsi

Supplier of motherboards, CPUs,
memory, add-on cards

Shopping Checklist

Chapter 7

Chapter 7

Shopping Checklist

So, you think you're ready to go shopping?

On the next pages, we've made a shopping list. This list will help you organize the features that you want for each of the major components in your system.

You may want to make multiple copies of this list.

CPU (circle desired processor)		Vendor A	Vendor B	Vendor C
Pentium processors				
P100 P120 P133 P150 P166 P200				
Cyrix 6x86 processors				
P100+ P120+ P133+ P150+ P166+		$_____	$_____	$_____

Motherboard select features	Motherboard A		Motherboard B		Motherboard C	
CPU speed to 200 MHz?	❏ Yes	❏ No	❏ Yes	❏ No	❏ Yes	❏ No
Maximum RAM to 128MB?	❏ Yes	❏ No	❏ Yes	❏ No	❏ Yes	❏ No
Handles EDO memory?	❏ Yes	❏ No	❏ Yes	❏ No	❏ Yes	❏ No
Bus type (PCI is recommended)	❏ PCI	❏ VLB	❏ PCI	❏ VLB	❏ PCI	❏ VLB
# of PCI or VLB slots						
# of ISA slots						
Cache memory capacity (min. 256K)	❏ Onboard	❏ Separate	❏ Onboard	❏ Separate	❏ Onboard	❏ Separate
I/O on MB or separate I/O card	❏ Onboard	❏ Separate	❏ Onboard	❏ Separate	❏ Onboard	❏ Separate
EIDE for 4 fixed drives	❏ Yes	❏ No	❏ Yes	❏ No	❏ Yes	❏ No
2 floppy drives	❏ Yes	❏ No	❏ Yes	❏ No	❏ Yes	❏ No
2 serial ports (16551 comp.)	❏ Yes	❏ No	❏ Yes	❏ No	❏ Yes	❏ No
I game port	❏ Yes	❏ No	❏ Yes	❏ No	❏ Yes	❏ No
I PS/2 mouse port	❏ Yes	❏ No	❏ Yes	❏ No	❏ Yes	❏ No
BIOS						
Plug 'n Play?	❏ Yes	❏ No	❏ Yes	❏ No	❏ Yes	❏ No
Flash?	❏ Yes	❏ No	❏ Yes	❏ No	❏ Yes	❏ No
Model						
Price	$_____		$_____		$_____	

Main memory RAM	Vendor A			Vendor B			Vendor C		
Type: 72-pin standard (FPM) 72-pin EDO	❏ FPM	❏ EDO		❏ FPM	❏ EDO		❏ FPM	❏ EDO	
Parity?	❏ Yes	❏ No		❏ Yes	❏ No		❏ Yes	❏ No	
Amount 8MB 2 x 4MB SIMMs	❏	❏	❏	❏	❏	❏	❏	❏	❏
16MB 2 x 8MB SIMMs	8	16	32	8	16	32	8	16	32
32MB 2 x 16MB SIMMs	MB	MB	MB	MB	MB	MB	MB	MB	MB
Price	$_____			$_____			$_____		

Cache memory (if not onboard)	Vendor A		Vendor B		Vendor C	
Type COAST or SRAM	❏ COAST	❏ SRAM	❏ COAST	❏ SRAM	❏ COAST	❏ SRAM
Capacity (usually 256K)						
Price	$_____		$_____		$_____	

CPU cooling fan	CPU Fan A	CPU Fan B	CPU Fan C
Model			
Price	$_____	$_____	$_____

Case	Case A		Case B		Case C	
Desktop or Tower	❏ Desktop	❏ Tower	❏ Desktop	❏ Tower	❏ Desktop	❏ Tower
Power supply (230 watt minimum)						
Price	$_____		$_____		$_____	

Keyboard	Keyboard A	Keyboard B	Keyboard C
Style			
Model			
Price	$_____	$_____	$_____

Mouse	Mouse A	Mouse B	Mouse C
Style			
Model			
Price	$_____	$_____	$_____

Video display card	Video card A			Video card B			Video card C		
PCI or VLB	❏ PCI	❏ VLB		❏ PCI	❏ VLB		❏ PCI	❏ VLB	
DRAM or VRAM	❏ DRAM	❏ VRAM		❏ DRAM	❏ VRAM		❏ DRAM	❏ VRAM	
Amount of video memory	❏ I MB	❏ 2 MB	❏ 4 MB	❏ I MB	❏ 2 MB	❏ 4 MB	❏ I MB	❏ 2 MB	❏ 4 MB
Model									
Price	$_____			$_____			$_____		

169

Monitor	Monitor A		Monitor B		Monitor C	
Screen size viewing area						
Dot pitch (.28 minimum)						
Refresh rate (70MHz minimum)						
Interlace or non-interlace	❏ Interlace	❏ NI	❏ Interlace	❏ NI	❏ Interlace	❏ NI
Maximum resolution (600 x 800 minimum)						
Energy saving features	❏ Yes	❏ No	❏ Yes	❏ No	❏ Yes	❏ No
Model						
Price	$_____		$_____		$_____	

Sound card	Sound card A		Sound card B		Sound card C	
Plug 'n' Play	❏ Yes	❏ No	❏ Yes	❏ No	❏ Yes	❏ No
Model						
Price	$_____		$_____		$_____	

Floppy drive	Floppy drive A		Floppy drive B		Floppy drive C	
3.5" drive	❏ Yes	❏ No	❏ Yes	❏ No	❏ Yes	❏ No
5.25" drive	❏ Yes	❏ No	❏ Yes	❏ No	❏ Yes	❏ No
Model						
Price	$_____		$_____		$_____	

IDE hard drive	IDE hard drive A	IDE hard drive B	IDE hard drive C
Capacity (1GB or higher)			
Access speed (12 ms or less)			
Model			
Price	$_____	$_____	$_____

IDE CD-ROM drive	IDE CD-ROM A	IDE CD-ROM B	IDE CD-ROM C
Access speed (4X speed or higher)			
Model			
Price	$_____	$_____	$_____

Software	Vendor A	Vendor B	Vendor C
MS-DOS 5 or 6.22 on diskette	$_____	$_____	$_____
Windows 95 on CD-ROM	$_____	$_____	$_____

171

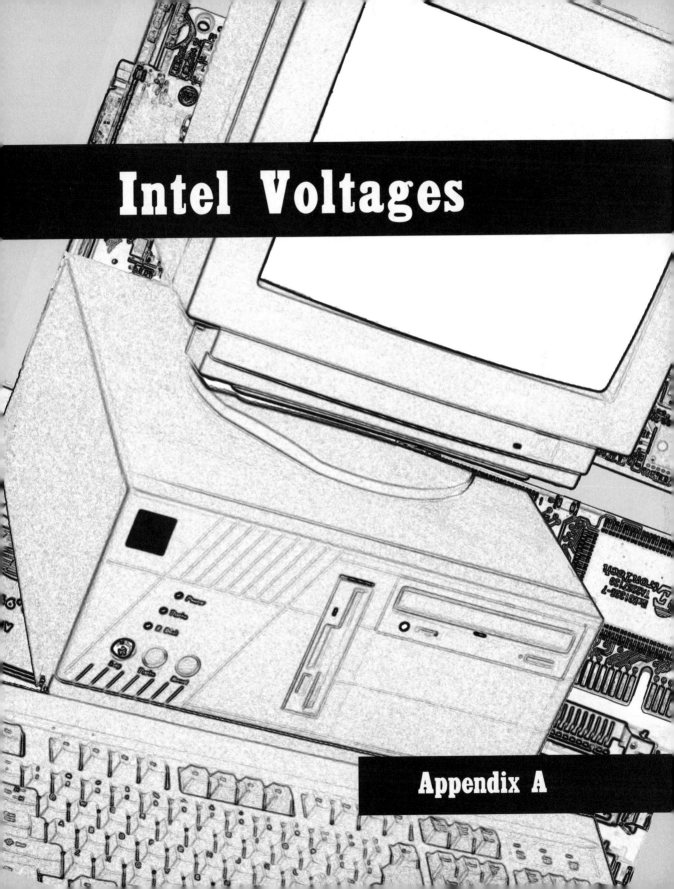

Intel Voltages

Appendix A

Intel Voltages

Appendix A, as we mentioned in Chapter 5, includes tables you can use to determine the voltage for Intel Pentium CPUs that do not have the three-letter suffix following the s-spec.

Again, if you have questions about the settings, ask the salesperson or technician from whom you bought the motherboard. They have a lot of experience building PCs and should be familiar with the specific settings for the motherboards they sell.

The following explains the abbreviations that are used in the tables:

Abbreviation	Voltage
STD	3.135V to 3.6V
VR	3.3V-3.465V
VRE	3.40-3.6V
MD	3.135V to 3.6V
VRE/MD	3.40-3.60V
DP	only used as a dual processor

S-Spec	Voltage	S-Spec	Voltage
SX879	STD	SX963	STD
SX885	MD	SZ996	STD
SX909	VR	SU032	STD
SX874	DP,STD	SK086	VRE/MD
SX886	MD	SX994	VRE/MD
SX910	VR,MD	SU033	VRE/MD
SX951	TCP Mobile	SX951	TCP Mobile
SX923	STD	SX923	STD
SX922	VR	SX923	STD
SX921	MD	SX922	VR
SX942	DP,STD	SX921	MD
SX943	DP,VR	SX942	DP,STD
SX944	DP,MD	SX943	DP,VR
SZ951	STD	SX944	DP,MD
SX960	VRE/MD	SZ951	STD
SX975	TCP Mobile	SX960	VRE/MD
SX961	STD	SX954	TCP Mobile
SZ977	STD	SX961	STD
SX957	STD	SZ977	STD
SX958	VR	SZ957	STD
SX959	MD	SX958	VR
SZ978	STD	SX959	MD
SX962	VRE/MD	SZ978	STD
SK079	TCP Mobile	SX962	VRE/MD
SX969	STD	SK079	TCP Mobile
SX998	MD	SX969	STD
SZ994	STD	SX998	MD
SU970	STD	SZ994	STD
SX968	STD	SU070	STD
SZ995	STD	SX968	STD
SU031	STD	SZ995	STD
SX970	VRE/MD	SU031	STD

S-Spec	Voltage	S-Spec	Voltage
SX970	VRE/MD	SK119	VRT,TCP
SX963	STD	SK122	VRT,SPGA
SZ996	STD	SK123	VRT,SPGA
SU032	STD	SK121	VRT,TCP
SK086	VRE/MD	SK124	VRT,SPGA
SX994	VRE/MD	SY020	TCP,VRT
SU033	VRE/MD	SY046	SPGA,3.1V
SK098	MD	SY021	TCP,VRT
SK089	VRT,TCP	SY027	SPGA 3.1V
SK091	VRP,SPGA	SY030	SPGA 3.3V
SK090	VRT,TCP	SY019	TCP,VRT
SK092	VRT,SPGA	SY028	SPGA 3.1V
SK110	STD/no Kit	SY009	TCP,Mobile
SK106	STD/no Kit	SY005	STD
SK106J	STD/no Kit	SU097	STD
SK107	STD	SU098	STD
SU038	STD/no Kit	SY006	STD
SY029	VRT,TCP	SY007	STD
SK113,V		SU110	STD
SK118	VRT,TCP	SU099	STD
SX999	3.3V, SPGA	SY033	STD
SY022	STD/no Kit	SU100	STD
SY023	STD		
SU073	STD/no Kit		
SY015	STD		
SU071	STD		
SY016	VRE/no Kit		
SY017	VRE		
SU072	VRE/no Kit		
SY037	VRE,PPGA		
SY044	VRE,PPGA		
SY045	VRE,PPGA		

177

Index

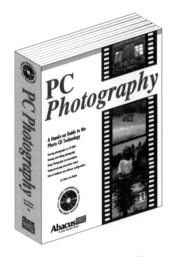

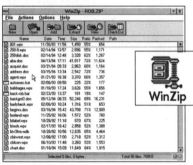

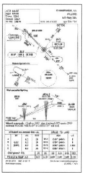